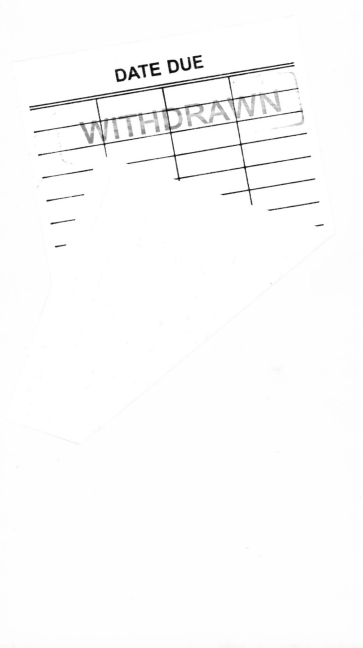

Fathers of Classical Music

By Charles Angoff, 1902

Illustrations by La Verne Reiss

Fathers of
CLASSICAL MUSIC

· *Essay Index Reprint Series*

BOOKS FOR LIBRARIES PRESS
FREEPORT, NEW YORK

STANDARD BOOK NUMBER:
8369-1119-9

LIBRARY OF CONGRESS CATALOG CARD NUMBER:
73-84294

PRINTED IN THE UNITED STATES OF AMERICA

Contents

Preface

THIS BOOK IS A SURVEY OF WESTern music from the days of Monteverdi up to the days of Haydn. Its special purpose is to show that such masters as Beethoven and Mozart and Schubert did not spring full-blown into being, that they built upon the work of their predecessors, and that these predecessors were men of high achievement.

To the best of my knowledge there is not in English a readable one-volume survey of this period in music. Indeed, there is very little, of a nature appealing to the general reader or the beginning student, that discusses the magnificent compositions of Corelli, Vivaldi, Couperin, and Rameau. One wishing to gain some idea about the character of these men and the quality of their work is hard put to it.

This volume attempts to fill this need. It makes no claim whatever to making any contribution to the history of the period. It is wholly a derivative work, based entirely upon the researches of others. I am the most amateurish of musicologists. My sole contributions are those of a popularizer (of a respectable order, I trust). I have attempted to bring together, within the space of a brief book, the best learning regarding a period in musical history that is full of magnificence but that has been neglected by all save the scholars who write for those already familiar, through long study and training, with this earliest era in musical annals. I do not think the riches of this era should be the exclusive property of the professionals.

The book is addressed to young students of music—in high school or the early years of college. The general reader with a broad cultural background should not find it beyond his comprehension. If a handful of readers of this modest book go on to further study of the glorious works of such men as Corelli and Vivaldi and Lully and Rameau and the two Scarlattis, and spread the good tidings of their discoveries, I shall be amply repaid.

CHARLES ANGOFF.

I

GENERAL INTRODUCTION

The Growth of Opera and the
Birth of the Symphony

THE WORK OF JOHANN SEBASTIAN
Bach did not only represent the beginning of an era. It also represented the culmination of an era. For some two hundred years preceding Bach's day a tremendous development in musical theory had been going on, and for an even longer period the art of musical composition, in the instrumental and vocal fields alike, had been undergoing vast changes. In other words, there were great musicians before Bach. In fact, it was Bach's predecessors who made his being, so to speak, possible. Some of these great predecessors of Bach were the following: Arcangelo Correli, Claudio Giovanni Monteverdi, Antonio Vivaldi, Alessandro and Domenico Scarlatti, Jean Philippe Rameau, Georg Friedrich Handel, Dietrich Buxtehude, and Christoph Willebald Gluck. Bach himself knew how truly great several of these men were. The violin concerti of Vivaldi, for example, had immense fascination for him, and he arranged many of them for the organ.

A quick glance at the history of music before the time of Bach and his musical progenitors will be helpful in placing them in perspective. There was, of course, music making as far back as human annals go. Vocal music making was perhaps the first form. When primitive man, out of sheer joy, imitated the roll of the waves or the pleasant sound made by the summer breeze, he was being musical. And when, by himself or as a member of a group, he lamented the cruelties of natural forces or the loss of a loved one, he also was being musical.

The voice was, and still is, man's most natural musical instrument, the most ancient and perhaps also most flexible and expressive at his command. Because of these qualities, and perhaps because of the accessibility of the instrument to all human beings, all religions have made use of it in their rituals. The Psalms form only one body of religious song. The Song of Solomon is another.

Music, instrumental and vocal, but especially the latter, constituted an important part of congregational religious services in the early Christian Church. For about three centuries, however, it seems to have been rather unorganized. It was only in the fourth century, A.D., that the church authorities attempted to bring some order into the singing at church services. St. Ambrose, the Bishop of Milan, was the first, according to most musicologists, who regulated the ecclesiastical singing in his diocese.

It was St. Ambrose who created a chant that has become known in musical history as the Ambrosian chant. It is the first recognizable ancestor of Western music. It is stately and solemn. While it is hard on the ears of modern listeners, it was employed in many churches for some two hundred years. It can still be heard in some of the more ancient Catholic churches of northern Italy.

Sometime in the seventh century the Papacy permitted a "humanization" of the Ambrosian chant. The result, known as the Gregorian chant, has been the foundation of Catholic church music down to the present. It is named after Pope Gregory the Great, who is said to have been the sponsor—some believe, the creator—of the chant. There are skeptics, however, who doubt the Pope had much interest in music at all.

In English the chant is generally known as "plain song." The French refer to it as "plain chant," while the Germans speak of it as "the choral." By whatever name it is known it has influenced music as few other factors have. The mightiest musicians have found inspiration in it—Johann Sebastian Bach, Mozart, Saint-Saëns, D'Indy, Respighi.

Despite the improvement of the Gregorian chant over the Ambrosian chant, it also is not easy to listen to, and the simple folk of the Middle Ages had the same difficulty. Some of the church composers sensed this and tried to liven up the chant with the melodies of folk-songs. These melodies were not always proper for church services, and often were vulgar and noisy.

The Sistine Chapel itself was not free of this vulgarity. Pope Nicholas V was greatly perturbed. He asked a cardinal to report upon the singing in the Sistine Chapel. The cardinal reported: "Methought I heard a herd of pigs grunting and squealing, for I could not understand a single word."

The scandal of church music finally became so great that at the Ecumenical Council of Trent, in 1564, the whole subject was discussed in great detail. Various suggestions were made by cardinals and chapelmasters, and all were presented to Pope Pius IV. The Pope appointed Cardinals Carlo Borromeo and Vitellozzo Vitellozzi as a committee of two to make specific proposals for the purification of church music.

The two cardinals called upon Giovanni Pierluigi da Palestrina (1514-1594), the distinguished musical master of the Liberian Chapel, to compose a model mass, one that would be simple, reverent, and in every way a worthy example of what church music should be.

Instead of writing one mass Palestrina wrote three. They were first heard at the palace of Cardinal Vitellozzi on Sunday, April 28, 1565. It was a historic day in the history of church music and of music in general. One of the masses was *Missa Papae Marcelli*, named after Pope Marcellus II, who had been a good friend of Palestrina's. It is one of the great monuments in the annals of music. Father Giuseppe Baini, Palestrina's first and still his best biographer, says of the mass:

"It is always well-balanced, always noble, always vivacious, always logical, always full of sentiment, always growing more powerful and lofty; the words easy to hear, the melodies suitable for prayer; the harmonies touching the heart, delightful and not disturbing; lovely with the loveliness of the sanctuary."

When Pope Pius IV first heard it he was moved to tears. He exclaimed to the many notables present, including almost the entire College of Cardinals:

"These must be the harmonies of the new song which the Apostle John heard in the triumphant Jerusalem, of which another John (Giovanni) gives us a foretaste in the pilgrim Jerusalem."

Palestrina's fame spread all over Europe. He is, in fact, the only composer, up to the end of the sixteenth century, whose works are still a living influence today. He wrote mainly masses, motets, or religious songs, and madrigals—more than thirty volumes of them. He was chiefly a composer of choir music. It includes some of the loftiest choir music ever put on paper.

No composer of church music since his day has been able to escape his shadow. Nearly every church service acknowledges the immortality of his work.

Serious musicians, throughout the Middle Ages and into the Renaissance, wrote much church music, less because of piety than because of the fact that in those days the approbation of the church authorities was at the same time the highest artistic praise. But the same composers who wrote masses also wrote for the new rising musical form of opera. Early in the seventeenth century music began to dominate lyrical tragedy more and more, and by 1650 the old recitative manner of stage conversation was reduced to a minimum, and it was relieved to a large extent by arias, dances and by choruses. The Roman aristocracy—for opera was chiefly an Italian phenomenon—now had a new plaything. Other centers of opera were Florence, Mantua and Milan. Paris also saw the production of opera in the middle of the seventeenth century, but on a far more modest scale.

The art of the musical came into being about this time. Apparently it first started as sheer burlesque, then it became a series of short tableaux with musical accompaniment, and then more elaborate libretti were written.

For long both opera and musical comedy were the sole pleasures of the upper classes, but actors and musicians soon discovered that they could be more continuously employed if they also appealed to the common people, who quickly revealed that they appreciated both opera and musical comedy as much as their social superiors. The first public theater for opera was opened in Venice in 1637.

Some of the prominent operatic composers of the time were Stefano Landi, Loreto Vittori, Vergilio Mazzochi, Marco Marazzoli, Luigi Rossi, Alessandro Scarlatti, Francesco Caletti Bruni, called Cavalli, and Claudio Giovanni Monteverdi. The last two are the most important.

The stock-in-trade of nearly all the librettists were cunning dodges, rapes, abductions, kidnaping and incestuous love, not to speak of adultery. These were usually spiced with withcraft and occasionally with astrology. The music generally was of a character to fit this melange—brash and tricky.

Cavalli was important in that he was one of the very first to bring some dignity into the opera houses. There are many stretches of sublimity in his operas, some of which are *Ercole Amante, Egisto, Scipione Africano,* and *Pompeo Magno.*

But Cavalli was also slipshod, and he often was as vulgar in his music as his librettists were in their tales. If he was occasionally capable of great rhythmic effects, he was also capable of vast stretches of dullness.

Monteverdi was a composer with enormously greater gifts and far more character. He was a master of the madrigal, a master of the dramatic cantata, and a master of the opera. He broke away from the pure polyphony of his contemporaries and predecessors and was one of the very first to make free use of extended melody. His arias have high passion, are instinct with genuine human feeling as distinguished from the bogus emotion of most operas of his day, and they have a being of their own. His opera *Orfeo* is a masterpiece in the history of music, and a milestone in the evolution of the operatic form.

Alessandro Scarlatti was, artistically, a minor Monteverdi. He was meticulous in the attention he gave to every section of his music, and he instituted important changes in the arrangement of the orchestra. He influenced Handel to a marked degree.

But the greatest advance in opera was made by Gluck. He more than anybody else lifted opera to the status of an art of the first order. When he entered upon the scene opera was still pretty much of a raffle barrel. Composers were the slaves of librettists and singers, particularly the latter. Singers considered themselves free to interpolate arias of their own composition into the score, in order to show off their vocal powers. With heroic effort—in *Orfeo* and *Alceste*—Gluck put a stop to this slavery of composers, and it was not long afterward that the opera-going public considered it bad manners for a singer to edit a score in any way. When that happened opera at last came of age.

The symphonic form is even more recent than the operatic form. It is, in fact, less than 200 years old. *Sinfonie* was the name given to the musical melange that introduced the opera. Soon it took on a life of its own and naturally fell into the sonata structure— announcement of theme, development, and recapitulation. Precisely how these transformations took place is still pretty much of a mystery, but the broad outlines of the development are fairly clear. The jump from the short symphony to the more elaborate work in the same form was made easily enough, and the more ingenious composers, in an obvious logical manner, began to write works now known as the sonata, the concerto and the suite.

In the original orchestra, it seems, the harpsichord was the leading instrument and the harpsichordist was also the conductor. There were few instruments in the earliest orchestras, which were often made up of no more than ten players—one, two, or three harpsichordists, one or two violinists, an oboeist, a bassonist, and a trumpeter. Clarinetists and trombone players were introduced by Mozart.

Since the early orchestras were so small there was little distinction between symphony music and chamber music. Indeed, several of those early symphonies are very short, which accounts for the fact that a man like Haydn could write about 125 symphonies without over-exertion, while Beethoven wrote only nine in a lifetime. Many of Haydn's symphonies were only short musical sketches.

No one knows how many of the early symphonies have been lost, and with them how much truly excellent music. The little that is discovered now and then is of astonishing beauty and grace. Some of the composers of this music were Giovanni Platti, Antonio Brioschi, E. F. Dall' Abaco, Matteo Alberti, Ferdinando Galimberto, Camerlocher, Fortunato Chelleri, Razetti, Paolo Salulini, G. B. Serini, Spurni and Andrea Zani.

In the words of Henry Prunières, the celebrated French musicologist and author of the excellent *A New History of Music:* "There is certainly talent in their music and often one comes across a beautifully turned page that might have been written by Haydn or the young Mozart."

Most of this early symphonic music was written by Italians, especially in Rome, Milan, and Venice. The Germans and Austrians did not achieve much prominence till toward the middle of the eighteenth century. Their music centers were Vienna and Leipzig.

The early orchestras, like the early operatic companies, were dependent upon the purse of a noble, who looked upon the players as his private entertainers.

Among the great instrumental masters of those days were Arcangelo Corelli, who wrote violin concerti and gavottes of almost otherworldly grace; Antonio Vivaldi, who belonged in the same class; Domenico Scarlatti, whose works for the harpsichord remain supreme in their field; Jean Philippe Rameau, who wrote many works for the harpsichord and the ballet that have endured for more than 250 years; Henry Purcell, François Couperin, Dietrich Buxtehude, and Jean-Baptiste Lully, one of the most facile and greatest composers of courantes, bourres, chaconnes, gigues, and minuets of all time.

Every one of these men exerted a profound influence on the giants of the late eighteenth century and nineteenth century—the Bachs, Mozart, Haydn, Beethoven, Brahms, Schumann, Schubert. It was by their mighty labors, completed about the middle of the eighteenth century, that the classical forms were set. They are the fathers of classical music.

These early composers did something else. They gave a new dignity to the life of the composer and even more so to his art. The curse of anonymity was the lot of the early composer as it was the lot of the early painter, sculptor and architect. He was, in a very real sense, the property of his patron, and his work was but the pleasure of him who paid for it.

During the Renaissance there was a rise in recogni-

tion of individuality in musical works, but when the
rule of absolute monarchy was imposed upon Europe
the composer was relegated again to the background
—and into anonymity. Musicians wrote to please
kings and princes, which is to say, they wrote showy,
extravagant music, for the level of taste among mon-
archs has generally been lowly.

With the French Revolution came a profound
change in the lot of the composer. The geniuses among
them took advantage of the mighty wave of demo-
cratic feeling, first to extricate themselves from their
subjection to the patronage of kings and nobles, and
second, to write from the depths of their own hearts.
Public orchestras sprang up everywhere, and with their
new public the composers felt liberated to write as
they pleased, guided only by their gifts and artistic
integrity.

Was the resulting music artistically of a high order?
For an answer one need only compare the work of,
say, Franz Schubert with the work of Lully. Indeed,
one need only compare the early work of Haydn with
his later work, written when he was no longer the
musical vassal of Prince Esterházy. The hand of
Haydn is in both groups of works, but the whole soul
of the man is to be found only in the later ones. What
is generally heard of Haydn's music in the concert
halls today are these later works.

II

Claudio Monteverdi

CLAUDIO MONTEVERDI WAS ONE of the great giants in the history of music, as an influence and probably also as an artist. Karl Nef, the eminent Swiss musicologist, says that "Monteverdi . . . may be placed beside his contemporary Shakespeare."

He was born in Cremona in May, 1567 or 1568, and as a very young man studied the new art of instrumentation. His first job, that of a viola player, was in the employ of the Duke of Mantua. The musical director for the duke was Marc Antonio Ingegneri, the prominent composer of church music. Monteverdi learned composition from him. In 1602 he succeeded Ingegneri as *maestro di capella* to the duke. Five years later he produced his first opera *Arianne*. It was a huge success. Its new and highly dramatic treatment of discords met with widespread favorable response.

Not many months afterward he presented to the public his second opera *Orfeo*, based upon the classic Greek legend of Orpheus and Eurydice. It was in

Orfeo that Monteverdi first made extensive use of pizzicato passages. He instructed the players: "Here you put down the bow and pull the strings with the finger."

Monteverdi was fortunate that about the same time the great violin maker Amati was in full production of his wonderful instruments, for the common violins of the day could not have rendered pizzicato passages with any grace.

In 1613 he was made *maestro di capella* at St. Mark's, Venice. There he wrote considerable church music, but most of it is lost. In 1632 he became a priest, but he wrote four more operas before he died on November 29, 1643. Perhaps the best of these last operas is *L'Incoronazione di Poppea*.

Monteverdi was the great embellisher of operatic music. In the words of Romain Rolland, "He belongs to the race of the colorists, that of Titian and Gabrielli." He was not an intellectual. He had no lofty message, as did Palestrina. To him music was, as Paul Landormy has said, "the most powerful means of expressing humanity, humanity as a whole with all its fears and desires, all its hopes and joys, all its deceptions and revolts." He pushed aside the calm and moderate rhythms of his day and introduced the *concitato*, or agitated, style. In other words, he brought the art of opera nearer to the commonplace emotions of everyday people.

He also lifted music from bondage to poetry. He said that " 'music does not confine herself merely to underlining the meaning of a text: she should look ahead,' and, beneath the words with which a character expresses his immediate thoughts or sentiments, should allow us to penetrate 'the past and the future of the personage' in question."

He abandoned the dry recitative, which was little more than inflected conversation, and substituted the melodic recitative, a free use of melody in long speeches, to give fluidity and color. This in itself was a historic innovation.

Monteverdi also gave a new dignity to the *da capo* air, or popular song, which he treated with skill in *Orfeo*.

In the same opera Monteverdi made use of what was for those days a very large orchestra, and which, in the words of Hugo Goldschmidt, may be termed the "apex and terminal point of ancient instrumentation." The orchestra was made up of thirty-six instruments: 2 *gravicembali* (clavecins), 2 *contrabassi de viola* (viol contrabasses), 10 *viol de brazzo* (arm viols), 1 *arpa doppia* (double harp), 2 *violini piccoli alla francese* (small French violins), 2 *chitaroni* (lutes), 2 *organ di legno* (wooden organs), 3 *bassi di gamba* (leg viols, held between the knees, like the 'cello), 4 *tromboni* (trombones), 1 *regale* (organ with reed stops), 2 *cornetti* (cornets, an obsolete sixteenth century form, with narrow mouthpiece of ivory or wood), 3 *trombe sordine* (trumpets with mutes), 1 *flautino alla vigesima seconda* (small flute), and 1 *clarino* (shrill-toned trumpet).

Monteverdi did not fare very well with a number of contemporary music critics. They were taken aback by his boldness of dramatic effects and his originality. His contemporary Artusi was especially violent in his denunciations of what he called Monteverdi's disregard of orthodox rules of composition and failure to distinguish between genuine harmony and sheer noise.

The people, however, found great pleasure in Monteverdi's operas, and his popularity had a considerable effect on the growth of opera in Italy and elsewhere in Europe. From 1637 to 1640 three huge opera houses were opened in Venice, and in the same period more than 350 operatic works were performed in them. In Bologna there was even greater operatic activity. Indeed, so popular did the form become that operas were performed, according to Paul Landormy, "even in convents," and at least one Pope, Clement IX, wrote an opera. Several cardinals served as librettists or stage managers.

Pope Innocent X was outraged by what was going on and set about to "regulate" opera. For this reason, or some other, decay set in, but not before the land had been filled with charm by the new musical inven-

Claudio Monteverdi

tion, which, according to Marco da Gagliano (1575-1642), composer of *Dafne*, produced the same year as Monteverdi's *Orfeo*, was "truly a spectacle for princes, admirable above all others, for in it are united all the most noble pleasures: poetic invention, drama, thought, style, sweetness of rhyme, charm of music, the concord of voices and instruments, the exquisite beauty of song, the grace of dance and gesture; even the attraction of painting in decoration and costume. And, finally, the intelligence and the loftiest emotions are charmed at one and the same time by the most perfected arts which human genius has invented."

The historic importance of Monteverdi's operas has been universally admitted, but their own high quality has been disputed. Charles Villiers Stanford has said of him: "The man is forgotten as a composer, and is only remembered as an innovator. He had his uses, not only as a pattern of what can be done, but as an example of what to avoid."

Sir Donald Francis Tovey has gone even further. Writing in the *Encyclopedia Britannica* he says: "A glance at the scores of some of Monteverdi's operas, or at the quotations given in musical histories, produces a disillusion unnecessarily great; we seem to be plunged into a more archaic period than that of the earliest efforts of polyphony. A modern stage performance restores the illusion. But an illusion it remains."

Many, perhaps most, critics disagree with both Stanford and Tovey. Prunières says that *Orfeo* "is beyond all question the masterpiece of the *Riforma Melodrammatica.*" Karl Nef says that Monteverdi's boldness in opera "astounds us even today. . . . Demonic and raging passion are at his disposal as easily as grace and most tender fervor."

Discussing the "Lamentation of Ariadne" in *Ariadne,* he says: "The elemental, changing rhythms, the harmonies thrown down like massive blocks, the serrated dissonances, are the factors which especially impress the listener. The freedom of the musical structure is unprecedented, especially in the treatment of dissonance. But inasmuch as the music expresses precisely what the composer wills, it is quite perfect, despite its being so thoroughly exceptional."

While there is some difference of opinion as to the artistic value of Monteverdi's operas, there is practically none regarding the value of his madrigals. Sir Donald Tovey says that Monteverdi's madrigals are an "achievement of something powerful and mature, which, if introduced into a madrigal concert, would make it impossible to continue the program with orthodox madrigals."

A madrigal is generally a secular—though sometimes a spiritual—composition for two or more voices, usually sung without instrumental accompaniment. The precise origin of the word is still pretty much of a mystery. Some say it is derived from a medieval Latin word signifying rustic song, others say that it was first a song to the Virgin Mary, while still others say that in the beginning it only referred to a short amorous or pastoral poem.

The first madrigals, apparently, were written in the middle of the fourteenth century, and generally consisted of two or three stanzas. During the following century the secular madrigals pretty much disappeared; the Vatican was inclined to frown upon them. The form was revived in the fourth decade of the sixteenth century. In Italy it remained to a large extent under the thumb of the church; Palestrina's spiritual madrigals are still among the glories of church music. It was, however, in Germany, the Netherlands and England that the secular madrigal achieved a high state. The madrigals of Hans Leo Hassler, Orlando di Lasso, William Byrd, Orlando Gibbons, Thomas Weelkes, John Wilbye, and John Ward can still be heard with much pleasure.

Monteverdi's teacher, Ingegneri, wrote beautiful madrigals, and it was, indeed, from him that Monteverdi learned a great deal about the art of madrigal writing. At the turn of the sixteenth century everybody with musical ambition tried his hand at madrigals. "Madrigals were written by every scribbler and the printers were unable to cope with the enormous supply."

With Monteverdi the art of madrigal writing probably reached its zenith. Where most of the other madrigalists inclined to insipidity and to broad and vague harmonic colors, Monteverdi introduced delicacy and quiet grandeur, bursting with vehemence, but it is the vehemence of the soul devoid of cheapness. In the words of Prunières, Monteverdi so transformed madrigal writing that "he conceived a new art." His "vehement art suggests Mozart and Beethoven; or again Corregio and the mighty Titian. Monteverdi, like the great Venetian painters of his time, Giorgione, Titian and Tintoretto, had that *certo fiammeggiare* of which Vasari speaks, a flaming passion usually held in check but which at moments is disclosed in its full elemental force."

III

Christoph Willibald Gluck

WHAT MONTEVERDI BEGAN IN the way of revolutionizing opera, Christoph Willibald Gluck developed to such a degree that he may with justice be called the father of modern opera. He struck the mightiest blow against the tradition that an opera was chiefly a means of displaying vocal technique—a tool to be used by tenors, sopranos, and basses—and thereby paved the way for Richard Wagner. Steeped in the philosophy of the Greek drama, he insisted upon the clear and simple in both libretto and music, and always his aim was to express sincere passions and deeply-felt sentiments. He made music the handmaiden of drama—perhaps too much so—and thus added intellectual stature to the burgeoning operatic form.

He also made enormous changes in the character and meaning of the overture. With him it was no more a mere "front-piece"; it was a summation of what follows, which sometimes performed its function so well that it achieved independent status.

Finally, he did not allow the ballet to interrupt the drama or the singing, as had previously been the case. He employed a ballet only when it fitted into the action, not as an intruder to give dancers a chance to reveal their skill.

The great musicologist, Dr. Paul Bekker, has summed up his importance in these words:

"His achievement consists in the fact that he thrust the doors open and allowed the daylight of human naturalness to fall upon the opera world of the time. In that light it was natural that many things should assume an aspect different from that which they had had under the half-light of the eunuch atmosphere that had hitherto obtained. Artistic virtuosity for its own sake gave way to a newly crystallizing purity of song. Reason and logic asserted their rights as men began to sing with their natural voices. Intellect and feeling of a clear and purified attitude toward art arose to form a critical conscience, which tested the art work for its possibilities in the light of the demands of a new ideal of form."

Gluck was born in Weidenwang, in the Upper Palatinate, on July 2, 1714. His father was game-keeper to Prince Lobkowitz, and in his boyhood he knew poverty and misery of soul. He was a choir boy in the Komotau Jesuit school, where he studied sing-ing, violin, organ, and clavecin. For a while he earned a precarious living as a wandering fiddler and singer in Prague. Then he studied 'cello under the Bohemian Czernohorsky, and became expert in the instrument.

When he was twenty-two he went to Vienna, where he impressed an Italian prince who took him to Milan. There Gluck studied for four years under Giovanni Battista Sammartini (1701-1775), composer of a great number of symphonies and string quartettes and one of Hadyn's celebrated predecessors. In April, 1741, Gluck made his debut as an operatic composer with *Artaserse*. It was a success. He wrote several others in quick succession, but hardly a trace of them remains. So many operas were written in those days that it was seldom thought worth while to preserve a copy of one. Gluck now had a reputation, but he was unhappy with the state of opera, including his own.

There were opera houses galore, but not a single work that was far removed from cheapness. Besides, the *castrato*, or male soprano, was the real master of what went on, not the librettist, or composer, or even the operatic manager. He obtained whatever "sympathetic" roles he wanted, and if he did not get them, he would not sing, and if he would not sing, there could be no performance. For the male soprano was the hero-lover of the time, as the tenor became later. Naturally, this tyrant got whatever costumes and props he desired—prancing horses, tall mountains, winding stairways, gorgeous headdress, fantastic canes.

The prima donna, of course, was no better. Her little page followed her on the stage, in all her scenes, including the most tragic. And the male soprano, when he finished his air, did not always leave the stage. Often he remained to watch the prima donna, or he walked around the stage eating fruit or drinking wine.

The behavior of the public was of a piece. According to Landormy, it "played cards or ate ices in the boxes, paying no attention to the stage unless some favorite air or some singer who was the fashion led people to turn their heads."

In 1745 Gluck went to London, where Georg Friedrich Handel was the king of the music world. Gluck produced two minor operas in the British capital; they were only mildly successful. In 1748 he went to Vienna where he produced his *Semiramide riconsciuta*. In the next twelve years he divided his time between Austria and Italy, and produced many operas, among them, *Ezio, L'Eroe cinese, Il Trionfo di Camillo, La Danza, Astigono, l'Isle de Merlin, l'Arbre enchanté, le Cadi dupe,* and *la Rencontre imprévue*.

Gluck's fame was rising. In 1754 he was made *Kappellmeister* of the Vienna Opera and in the same year the Pope made him a knight of the Golden Spur.

About this time Gluck met Raniero da Calsabigi

(1714-1795), who had edited the poetical works of Metastasio, who had supplied the libretti to nearly all Italian composers, and also to Gluck. Calsabigi and Gluck probably decided upon a collaboration when they met in Vienna in 1761. The product of their collaboration, *Orfeo ed Euridice*, was first performed at the Burgtheater in Vienna on October 5, 1762. Gluck and Calsabigi had rehearsed their company as they had never been rehearsed before.

A most distinguished audience was present at the first performance. The Austrian nobility was well represented, and Empress Maria Theresa herself was present. They found the opera something of a disappointment. There were only four characters, if the chorus is counted as one, and the story was bare almost to austerity. The music was simple and graceful, but there were only two or three arias in the current style.

There was, of course, also tone painting of a most marvelous kind, and the music and the drama fitted so well together that each gave the other a new shade of meaning. The opera did not reach the popular success it merited till some years later. Henry Chorley has said of it: "There is no opera in the world's long list, which, with merely three female voices and a chorus, can return to the stage in days like ours to make the heart throb and the eyes water."

The people of Vienna had witnessed a revolution

in the history of opera. To whom is the chief credit
due? Gluck himself was clear enough on this point.
Twelve years later he wrote:

"I should reproach myself still more, were I to
allow the invention of the new kind of Italian opera,
whose success has justified the experiment, to be
attributed to me. It is to M. Calsabigi that the credit
is mainly due."

Calsabigi elaborated upon this matter. Since his
remarks are musicologically interesting, it is here
given at some length:

"I am no musician, yet I have long studied declamation. It is acknowledged that I have a talent for
reciting verses well, especially tragic poems and, above
all others, my own. Twenty-five years ago I thought
that the only music suitable for dramatic poesy, above
all for dialogue, and for those airs which we call airs
with action, was that which would most closely
approximate *natural declamation*, animated and ener-
getic; that declamation itself was no more than a kind
of imperfect music; that it might be set down in notes
as it exists had we been able to find a sufficient number
of signs to express so many tones, so many inflections,
so many stresses and softenings, the shadings, infinitely
varied, so to speak, which the voice assumes when
declaiming. . . .

"I arrived in Vienna in 1761 filled with these ideas.
One year later, His Excellency Count Durazzo, then

director of the spectacles of the Imperial Court, and today ambassador to Venice, to whom I had recited my *Orfeo*, induced me to give it to the stage. I consented, on condition that its music would be written according to my wish. He sent Signor Gluck to me, who, so he said, would oblige me in all respects. . . . I read my *Orfeo* to him, and recited several fragments, again and again, pointing out the shadings, the nuances I wished to put into my declamation, the suspensions, the tempos, the sounds of the voice, at times full, at others enfeebled and negligible, which I desired him to employ in his composition. At the same time I begged him to dispense with the *passaggi*, the *cadenze*, the *ritornelli*, and whatever of the Gothic, the barbarous, and the extravagant had been introduced into our music. Signor Gluck entered into my views."

In a larger sense the credit for the revolution in opera really belongs to the logic of history. The "new" ideas had already been proposed and, in part, realized by Lully, Rameau, and, of course, Monteverdi. Gluck, aided by Calsabigi, merely developed these ideas more fully than any composer had previously done.

On December 16, 1766, the second work of the Gluck-Calsabigi collaboration was given to the world in Vienna. It was called *Alceste*, and represented an even bolder handling of the new ideas. This is the opera with the dramatic Chorus of the Spirits and the famous aria "Divinités du Styx." Years later Wagner spoke of this opera with reverence, but the contemporary public cared little for it. A few discerning listeners, however, saw its grandeur. A Gluck admirer exclaimed: "I am in a wonderland: a serious opera without a male soprano (*castrato*), music without solfeggio exercises, or rather without 'garglings,' an Italian poem without bombast and witticisms, such is the triple prodigy with which the Court Theater opens!"

Gluck still had to score a success for his new ideas with his contemporary musical world. He abandoned Vienna and sought better fortune in Paris, where he at least had the interest of a one-time pupil, Marie Antoinette. In collaboration this time with Bailli du Roullet, who wrote the libretto, Gluck presented *Iphigénie en Aulide* at the Paris Opera on April 19, 1774.

The first performance was coldly received, but the second brought forth almost unanimous praise. Marie Antoinette wrote: "At last a great triumph! . . . I was carried away by it. We can find nothing else to talk about. You can scarcely imagine what excitement reigns in all minds with regard to this event. It is incredible."

Among the famous elements in this opera are the overture, the ballet music, the march, and the baritone aria, "Diane impitoyable!"

Christoph Willibald Gluck

The success of *Iphigénie en Aulide* reached such magnitude that there was a demand to hear *Orfeo*. The opera was slightly altered, and the first performance of the new version took place on August 2, 1774. The acclaim was boundless. The great critic J. J. Rousseau said: "When one can enjoy so great a pleasure for two hours, then I can conceive of life's being worth living!"

Two years later a new French version of *Alceste* was presented in Paris. It was a failure, but Gluck apparently was not too perturbed. At least he had prepared himself for the eventuality of failure when he said:

"It would be amusing were this work to fall a failure. . . . *Alceste* is not meant merely to please our own day, and because of its novelty is a timeless work; I may say that it will please equally well two hundred years from now, if the French language does not change, and I say so because I have built its foundations only on nature, which is never subject to fashion."

Despite setbacks Gluck's reputation seemed to be established, but his enemies were not done with him. La Harpe and Marmontel continued to attack him and his theories, and for a long time they and others of a like mind were looking for a musician they could play off against him. They finally agreed on Nicola Piccinni (1728-1800), a talented composer of amazing musical fecundity. He wrote at least 127 stage works, most of which were successful. Perhaps the most popular of these was *Cecchina* or *La Buona figliuola* (*The Good Girl*). A comic opera, written in the Neapolitan style, it won for Piccinni great wealth and fame. A lean, sickly, gentle, weary little man, he was almost literally thrown in the ring to do battle with Gluck.

He came to Paris on the last day of 1776. He knew so little French that Marmontel had to give him lessons. Everything was now set for the battle between the Gluckists and the Piccinnists. Gluck wrote *Armide*, which was a success. The next year Piccinni offered his *Roland*, "upon which he had been working since his arrival in Paris, and which was awaited with impatience by the public. On the day of the premiere Piccinni no longer looked like a human being. His wife and son were sobbing, and he sobbed in unison with them."

The opera was a success. The Gluckists and Piccinnists were exactly where they had started. Whereupon it was decided to ask Piccinni to do an *Iphigénie en Tauride*, to show off against Gluck's opera of the same name. Gluck's was performed in 1779, bringing forth much enthusiasm. Piccinni's was presented two years later. The first two acts were coldly received, but the third impressed the audience.

At the second performance of Piccinni's *Iphigénie* a fateful thing happened. The second leading singer was so intoxicated that she committed many blunders. The audience was shocked to anger. A wit who was present exclaimed, "This is no *Iphigénie en Tauride.* This is *Iphigénie en Champagne!*" This established the failure of the opera, and thereafter Gluck's *Iphigénie* alone was to be seen. The Gluckists were triumphant. Gluck was victor.

But there was little pleasure in the victory for the sixty-five-year-old composer. He saw no point in the battle to begin with. He could not forgive the Parisians for making his life so difficult, for being so slow in recognizing his contributions. He left Paris in 1779 and never composed another major work of opera. His faculties were declining, his body was racked with a multitude of ailments. He was glad he was back in Vienna, where he died on November 15, 1787. On his tomb was inscribed this epitaph:

"Here lies an honest German, a good Christian and a faithful husband, Christoph Willibald Ritter von Gluck, a master of the art of music, who died November 15, 1787."

Piccinni, to his glory, delivered the public eulogy. To his even greater glory he urged the musical world to show its homage to the memory of Gluck by giving a concert of his works every year. The vow has not been kept. This only places Gluck in the company of nearly all the great artists in every form at all times and all places.

Piccinni himself came upon evil days. He returned to Naples, where he was accused of "liberalism." He decided to go to Venice, returned to Naples, and then journeyed back to Paris. The Directory voted him a pension but seldom paid it. He died in poverty on May 7, 1800, at Passy. He deserved a better fate, for he had skill, facility, and occasional touches of genius. According to Landormy, "He was a genuine musician, who sometimes makes us think of Mozart, but more especially of Rossini."

Gluck's contribution to opera was so great that it is worth while returning to an assessment of it. But first it is well to read what he himself said in his "Dedicatory Epistle to the Grand Duke of Tuscany," which appears upon the score of *Alceste:*

"When I undertook to set to music the opera *Alceste,* it was my intention to avoid all the abuses which the misunderstood vanity of singers and the excessive complaisance of composers had introduced into Italian opera and which, from the most magnificent and beautiful of all spectacles, has turned it into the most tiresome and ridiculous. I sought to bring back music to her veritable function, that of seconding poetry, of strengthening the expression of the sentiments, and the interest of the situations, without inter-

rupting the action or chilling sympathy with super-
fluous ornament. I believed that music should add to
poetry that which a correct and well-planned design
lends to vivacity of color and the happy agreement
of lights and shadows, which serve to animate figures
without changing their outlines.

"Hence I have taken care not to interrupt a singer
in the midst of his dialogue to make him wait for a
wearisome *ritornelle*, or to stop him in the middle of a
speech on a favorable vowel, either to deploy the
agility of his fine voice in an extended passage, or to
wait for the orchestra to give him time to draw breath
to make an organ-point.

"Nor have I thought necessary either to pass rapidly
over the second part of an air, when this second part
is the most impassioned and important, in order to
repeat the words of the air regularly four times; nor
end the air before the meaning is completed, to give
the singer a chance to prove that he can vary a passage
to suit his taste in several different ways.

"Finally, I wished to proscribe all these abuses
which, for so long a time, good sense and good taste
have in vain decried.

"It seems to me that the overture should inform the
spectators in advance with regard to the character of
the action about to enroll before their eyes, and to
indicate to them its subject; that the instruments
should be brought into play only in a manner propor-

tionate in degree to the interests and passions involved; that above all it would be necessary in the dialogue, to avoid too sharp a discrepancy between the air and the recitative, in order not to destroy the meaning of the sentence, nor willfully interrupt the movement and ardor of the scene out of season.

"I also thought that the greater part of my labor should be confined to seeking a beautiful simplicity, and I have avoided a display of difficulties at the expense of clarity; I have attached no importance to the discovery of a novelty, unless it were one naturally offered by the situation and bound up with the expression; finally, there was no rule which I did not think might be sacrificed with good grace for the benefit of the effect."

In other words, Gluck was for simplicity, clarity, and integrity. He was against cheapness, flamboyance, and complexity. That is why he favored ancient themes for his works, for they were above contemporary prejudices and fashions. No wonder Gluck was so disliked in France. The lyric tragedy there was a false one—contemporary, sentimental, insipid, vague, intricate, sensual, and brashly spectacular. It reflected the decaying society of the times. Gluck's honesty and simplicity seemed boorish to the French courtiers and their flunkies.

Gluck gave tragedy its true significance. He was

truly the father of modern lyric tragedy. Richard Wagner himself never forgot that.

Unlike Lully and Rameau, Gluck always kept his head and heart close to genuine human emotions and ideas. Everything he put on paper had a compelling reason within; it was never influenced by the consideration of "foreign" likes or dislikes. What a king or a queen wanted in a musical work was his or her private wish; Gluck did not treat such a wish even as a request.

Sometimes, Gluck went too far in his devotion to his principles. He once declared, "Before beginning an opera, I make but one prayer, to forget that I am a musician."

This fanaticism perhaps accounts for the stretches of "melodious declamation" in several of Gluck's operas.

In Gluck's search for simplicity he often sank into dryness. "His melody lacks Italian abundance and Mozartean ease."

Then, in his search for worthy themes for opera, he at times became too lofty—and even a bit pompous. Human beings like to look at the sky, but they also like to look at the earth—and sometimes they like to look at other human beings about them. They yearn for perfection but they like to return to imperfection. There they find familiarity and warmth and comfort. Gluck did not always remember that.

These criticisms are noted out of fairness to those who were not too impressed by Gluck in his own day. They are minor criticisms. They are hardly blemishes upon the memory of one of the giants in the history of music.

IV

Alessandro and Domenico Scarlatti

ALESSANDRO AND DOMENICO SCAR-
latti were father and son and
each made a major contribution to musical history.
Domenico was perhaps a greater artist than his father,
but the father was of considerable importance himself. Alessandro Scarlatti was born in Palermo, Sicily,
in 1659. He was a pupil of Giacomo Carissimi
(1604-1674), a celebrated organist, choirmaster and
writer of oratorios.

He was master of the chapel of the Queen of
Sweden in Rome in 1680, and four years later was
made conductor of the royal company of musicians in
Naples. In 1703-1708 he was master of the chapel
at Santa Maria Maggiore in Rome. He wrote a great
deal of chamber music and church music, especially
for gatherings of the Accademia della Arcadia, where
he made the acquaintance of Corelli, Pasquini,
Francischiello, and Handel. In 1709 he was made the
director of the Conservatory of the Poor of Jesus
Christ, and he died on October 24, 1725.

He wrote about 120 operas, 200 Masses, 700 cantatas, and an indeterminate number of oratorios, madrigals, etc. While not popular in his own time—he was called "the serious Scarlatti"—he was without question the most famous representative of the Neapolitan school of opera.

The Neapolitan school put the emphasis on music as the superior of drama or poetry. This school held a dominating position at the end of the seventeenth and at the beginning of the eighteenth century. Among the founders of the school were Francesco Provenzale (1610-1704), an operatic composer of more than local fame, and Alessandro Stradella (1645-1682).

The heart and soul of Neapolitan opera was the aria. As a matter of fact, in the words of Karl Nef, the Neapolitan operas were "veritable series of arias, linked together by means of recitative. The aria evolved as a formal, strictly organic whole from the originally free effusion of realistic musical declamation in the oldest operas. Of course, this evolution did not take place with one bound, but gradually. Alessandro Scarlatti brought it to a conclusion."

The aria is a three-part form, *a b a*. It reached its zenith in the eighteenth century, and was used by Handel, Bach, Gluck, and Mozart, to mention only a few composers of the highest rank. At first the sense of form exemplified by the aria was the very heart of

Alessandro Scarlatti

opera. It was, indeed, sought after as a good in itself,
and rapidly removed itself from life.

This does not mean, of course, that all arias were
largely artificial. Some of them, like those by Alessandro Scarlatti, were of sublime beauty and brimming
with emotion. But even Scarlatti tended more and
more to be formal rather than passionate in his arias,
and sheer musical architecture tended to predominate.
Which is why "the Neapolitan school brought the
vocal solo to its highest perfection." Arias are the food
and drink of singers, and the more architecturally perfect they are the better singers like them.

The singers did more than render superbly the arias
written for them. They were expected to embellish
the arias in the repeats, and he who introduced the
most effective embellishments and at the same time
kept within the spirit of the original was adjudged an
artist of high order. Male sopranos achieved considerable fame with their embellishments. Among these
castrati were Farinelli, Senesino, Bernacchi, and
Manzuoli.

The freedom given to singers had overwhelming
disadvantages. It was, indeed, a menace to the integrity of musical art. Singers tended to substitute bravura
for expression, and sensational facility took the place
of real art. It was not long before decay and corruption
set in.

"Scarlatti himself was still far removed from the

weaknesses with which the later Neapolitan opera was justly charged. His style is more fluent and more vocal, as well as more charming, than that of J. S. Bach; at the same time it is scarcely less solid. He was a master of form and of counterpoint, and at the same time a fine portrayer of character. His works," continues Karl Nef, "will remain models for all time."

Scarlatti's interest in sheer music (as the superior of drama and poetry) was so great that he lavished enormous skill, not only upon the composition of arias, but also upon his operatic overtures, or *sinfonias*. His overture was generally a three-part work, an allegro, an adagio or an andante, and again an allegro. This form later became the basis of what is now known as the symphony, a work of independent and massive significance. The sonata and the concerto also adopted it. Alessandro Scarlatti is thus, in a very profound sense, the father of modern instrumental music. His operas are forgotten, save perhaps a few arias and *sinfonias*, but his influence was monumental.

The magnitude of Domenico Scarlatti as a writer of symphonies, as a composer for the harpsichord, and as an orchestral technician is of historic proportions. As an inventor of new forms of instrumental music he was probably the superior of Johann Sebastian Bach and Georg Friedrich Handel, though he was their inferior in content. Perhaps even more than

Domenico Scarlatti

his father he heralded the coming of the sonata, and in his playing of the harpsichord he was probably one of the greatest virtuosi of all time.

He was born in Naples in 1685 and died there in 1757. He studied under his father, of course, and also under Gasparini and, very likely, Gaetano Greco. His original and highly imaginative playing of the harpsichord did not appeal much to the Italians of his day, for they were steeped in opera and cared little for anything else in the realm of music. In 1708 he met Handel, probably in Rome, where Cardinal Ottoboni arranged a harpsichord contest between the two. Some historians say that Scarlatti was the winner. But when a similar contest on the organ was arranged, Scarlatti openly admitted that Handel was his superior by far; in fact, Scarlatti added, he had not thought such sublime organ playing was possible in the world. The two became lifelong friends and were frequently seen together.

In 1709 Scarlatti entered the service of the Queen of Poland, and he wrote several operas for her private theatre in Rome. Among these operas were: *Sylvia*, *Orlando*, *Ifigenia in Aulide*, *Ifegenia in Tauride*, *Narciso*, and *Hamlet;* the last was perhaps the first musical setting of that subject anywhere.

In 1715 Scarlatti was made musical director of St. Peter's Church, Rome. Four years later he was in London, and in 1721 he was engaged in musical ac-

tivities in the court of Lisbon. In 1729 he moved to
the Spanish court, where he was music master to the
Princess of the Asturias. In 1754 he returned to
Naples and remained there for the last three years of
his life.

He composed ten operas, which are virtually forgotten, a Stabat Mater, and about 350 harpsichord
pieces, which have earned him immortality. The entire harpsichord output is edited by Ricordi.

Scarlatti called his harpsichord pieces *Essercizi*.
The earlier ones were probably what we would now
call études, but nearly all were built in what is now
called the sonata form, and their influence upon future
pianoforte composition is incalculable. He inaugurated a new era in the playing of keyboard instruments—crossing of hands, arpeggios, runs.

Above all, he brought a new language to music by
making the harpsichord speak in a manner that was
fresh, rich, and varied. C. Hubert Parry has said:

"His instincts for the requirements of his instrument were so marvelous, and his development of technique so wide and rich, that he seems to spring full-
armed into the view of history. . . . He knew well
the things that will tell, and how to awaken interest
in a new mood when the effects of any particular line
are exhausted. Considering how little attention had
been given to technique before his time, his feats of
agility are really marvelous. The variety and incisive-

ness of his rhythms, the peculiarities of his harmony, his wild whirling rapid passages, his rattling shakes, his leaps from end to end of the keyboard, all indicate a preternaturally vivacious temperament; and unlike many later virtuosos, he is thoroughly alive to the meaning of music as an art, and does not make his feats of dexterity his principal object. . . . He left behind him a most copious legacy to mankind. . . ."

V

Jean Baptiste Lully, Jean Philippe Rameau,
Francois Couperin, Henry Purcell,
Giovanni Battista Pergolesi

THERE WERE, OF COURSE, OTHER composers of opera and instrumental music in the general class of the Scarlattis. Not all of them can be discussed or even mentioned in this volume, but a few deserve consideration here. Jean Baptiste Lully was a very distinguished composer of opera and of instrumental pieces, and his arrangement of the orchestra, with its emphasis upon the string section, clearly foreshadowed the modern orchestra with its balanced sonorities. In his day he was a personage of the highest importance, and historically he occupies a place of much distinction.

He was born in Florence on November 29, 1632, and died in Paris on March 22, 1687. At the age of ten he was taken to France by the Chevalier de Guise to present him to his niece, Mlle. de Montpensier. For a while he worked in her household as a kitchen hand, but the Chevalier also had him study music. Lully quickly lost interest in his kitchen work, and it was not long before he was dismissed by the noble-woman.

He became a virtuoso violinist and founded the *Bandes des petits violons*, helped greatly by Louis XIV, who took an interest in him. Lully now took up composition in a serious way and studied with Nicholas Mertu, François Roberdet, and Gigault. At twenty-five he married a rich woman, thereby assuring himself financial security the rest of his life.

With Molière he wrote several ballets, and then he established a historic collaboration with Quinault, with whom he composed the first legitimate French opera, *Les Fêtes de l'Amour et de Bacchus*, which was first presented on November 15, 1672. Quinault and Lully had an arrangement by which they were to write an opera a year for fourteen consecutive years. They kept to their agreement, but Lully went beyond the goal he set himself. He composed an additional six operas in that period of time, or twenty operas in all.

In addition to operas Lully also wrote much sacred music, including several motets for double choir, which were published in 1684. It was, indeed, while conducting one of his religious compositions, a Te Deum, in January, 1687, that he accidentally struck his foot with the baton, thus inducing blood poisoning, from which he died two months later. He left three sons, Louis, Jean Baptiste, and Jean Louis, all of

Jean Baptiste Lully

whom were musicians of standing, but none of them had any real talent.

Lully was first and foremost a formalist, a designer, in other words, an intellectual composer. This is not to say he was without feeling; he had much of that, but it was superficial feeling, highly pleasurable, in line with the sensual atmosphere of the court of Louis XIV. He was the classical composer of the late seventeenth and eighteenth century, that is, the classical French composer.

There was little genuine elevation in him, but he had great skill, and the establishment of the "French overture" must probably be credited more to him than to anybody else. Bach and Handel learned much from him.

Among his better known works are the following: *Cadmus et Hermione* (1672), *Alceste* (1674), *Atys* (1676), *Isis* (1677), *Proserpine* (1680), *le Triomphe de l'Amour* (1681), *Roland* (1685), *Armide et Renaud* (1686) and *Acis et Galatée* (1687).

Jean Philippe Rameau was the great colorist of French music, as Lully was the great formalist. The difference between the two was the occasion of a historic musical battle, known as the *guerre des bouffons*. It foreshadowed by many years the more important battle between the Gluckists and the Piccinnists.

Rameau was born in Dijon on September 23, 1683,

and died in Paris on September 12, 1764. His father
was an organist, who knew privation, and wanted his
son to be a magistrate. But Rameau had different aims
in life. Indeed, his love of music was so great that,
it is said, he could play almost any musical composition on sight. First with his father, and then with
other teachers, he studied the harpsichord, the organ,
and the violin. At seventeen he had an affair with a
widow, which somewhat interfered with his musical
education, but it also had one good effect: his father
sent him to Italy in the hope that the trip would help
to get the widow out of his son's mind. Apparently,
the trick worked, for Rameau plunged into a study of
composition and playing in Italy, though he never
did learn to spell acceptably.

In 1702 he was made temporary music director of
the Metropolitan Church in Avignon, and in 1708
• he succeeded his father at the Church of Notre Dame,
where he was for five years. He then played at the
Jacobins, Lyons, and at the Cathedral in Clermont-
Ferrand. It was while at the last that he wrote the
celebrated treatise, *Traité de l'harmonie,* which was
published in 1722.

Altogether he wrote thirty operas and ballets and
a number of harpsichord works. His best known operas
were *Hippolyte et Aricie,* which was first performed
at the Paris Opera in 1733, and *Castor et Pollux,* first

Jean Philippe Rameau

performed at the same opera house in 1737. Rameau also wrote cantatas and chamber works.

Rameau was equally prominent as a performer, theorist, and composer. He codified the principles of classical harmony. In a very real sense, Rameau—despite the battle between his admirers and those of Lully—was only a follower of Lully. To be sure, he inclined more to color, yet he, too, did not center his attention on emotion. Both imitated nature, as Landormy shrewdly points out, and both were chiefly interested in describing the outside world.

"Rameau, falling into a decline with years, said of himself," according to Landormy, " 'From day to day I gain in taste, but I no longer possess genius!' It is possible that he always had more taste than genius."

The Couperin family has been celebrated in music from as far back as 1626 down to the time of Mlle. Céleste Couperin, organist at St. Gervais, who died in 1850. The most famous of them, however, was François Couperin, which is why he is generally referred to as Le Grand Couperin.

His life was quite uneventful. He was born in Paris on November 10, 1668, and died there on September 12, 1733. In 1693, at the age of twenty-five he was made *organist du roi* and in 1717 he was made *Ordinaire de la musique de la chambre du roi.* He remained at the latter post till his death. He was or-

ganist at the Church of St. Gervais in Paris from
1685 till his death in 1733. Nearly all his life he
enjoyed the patronage of Louis XIV.

Though chiefly a secular instrumentalist, Couperin
also wrote much church music. Among his works in
this class are: *Motets pour l'Élévation, Versets de Motets, Motet de Sainte-Suzanne* and *Leçons de Ténèbres.*

His place in history rests solidly on his almost otherworldly harpsichord pieces—*Pièces de Clavecin*—of
which he wrote four volumes, 1713, 1716, 1722,
1730. He also wrote *Art de toucher le clavecin,* 1717,
and *Apothéose de l'incomparable Lully.* His trios for
two violins and bass were the first such trios to be
introduced in France.

His harpsichord suites—all enormously admired
by Johann Sebastian Bach—are mostly programmatic,
and indeed are picturesquely titled. He said:

"In composing I always have a particular subject
before my eyes. Various circumstances always suggest
to me this, and also my titles."

Some of the titles of his dance pieces are: *Fanfare
for Diana's Procession, The Foresters, The Bees, The
Carillon of Cytherea, The Little Nuns, The Lady
with the Waving Plumes, Tender Languors,* and
Happy Thoughts.

For elegance, for finesse, for charm, for sheer
magic there is probably no composer in world history
to compare with Couperin. He was perhaps even more

François Couperin

miraculous than Mozart. His grace and tenderness are as mysterious in their power as they seem to be mystic in their origin. No one in his senses has ever said a harsh word against Couperin's music, as no one in his senses has ever said a harsh word against the summer breeze or a November evening.

His works, to be fully appreciated, must be heard on his own instrument, the harpsichord. Perhaps that is why Wanda Landowska, the incomparable harpsichordist, is perhaps best fitted to sing the praises of Couperin as they should be sung:

"Couperin created a style and technique of his own. Like Chopin, Couperin is great not only for what he brings to his instrument by way of creative gifts, but also in what he draws from it. The resources of the instrument are wonderfully extended and immeasurably enriched by this early French master, who must be considered one of the earliest great composers of the keyboard. . . . One finds in his pieces for the harpsichord that sustained and full lyric line, those strong and appealing harmonies, that intensity of expression, that richness of atmosphere, all of which are qualities belonging to him."

Henry Purcell, the "father of English music," was born in Westminster probably in 1659 and died there in 1695. He may, with justice, be called the John Keats of English music. At his loveliest—especially in his songs—he has never been surpassed, save perhaps by Schubert. Though he lived only about thirty-seven years, he was a prolific composer. The Purcell Society has brought together twenty-two volumes of his works in every form: operas, odes, masques, chamber music, harpsichord and organ pieces, trios, and duets.

Among his teachers were his uncle Thomas Purcell, Pelham Humphrey, and particularly the organist Dr. John Blow, who wielded a powerful influence on him. In 1677 he was appointed "composer in ordinary for the violin" to the King, and three years later he succeeded Dr. Blow as organist at Westminster Abbey.

His most celebrated opera, *Dido and Aeneas*, was first performed at the Josias Priest School for Girls in Chelsea about 1689. Some of the other operas he wrote are *Dioclesian*, *Tyrannic Love*, *Amphitryon*, *King Arthur*, *Don Quixote*, and *The Indian Queen*. The song in *King Arthur*, "Fairest Isle," is still sung in music schools.

Some of Purcell's other well-known songs are: "Swifter, Isis, swifter flow," "St. Cecilia," "O I was glad," and "My heart is inditing." He also wrote songs for Spenser's *The Faerie Queene*.

Two of his better known works in the realm of church music are *Te Deum* and *Jubilate* for St. Cecelia's Day, 1694.

Henry Purcell

In addition to numerous masterpieces for the harpsichord Purcell wrote several *Fantasias* for strings that
are original, fresh, bold, and utterly captivating. His
Golden Sonata alone, written for two violins and
harpsichord, would have assured him immortality.

Dido has been played all over Europe and has also
been performed in America. It is perhaps the first
great opera in English—and possibly the only one to
date. According to Gustav Holst, it is "one of the
most original expressions of genius in all opera."

The libretto, written by Nahum Tate, is based upon
the love story of Dido and Aeneas from Virgil's
Aeneid. The music is subordinate to the book, but it
has independent value and gives the tale a sublimity
it lacks in itself. The music is vivid, descriptive in a
highly pictorial way, yet not brash; it is direct, and
the ballet is not an interruption but an integral part
of the play. "Dido's Lament" at the end of the opera
is one of the most moving laments in all musical
literature.

Mention must be made of Giovanni Battista Pergolesi, generally called the father of comic opera
(opera-buffa). He lived only twenty-six years (1710-
1736), yet he managed to write several operas, a
Stabat Mater, and small pieces for orchestra.

His masterpiece, *La Serva Padrona (The Maid
Rules the Master)*, was first performed at the Teatro

Giovanni Battista Pergolesi

San Bartolommeo in Naples on August 28, 1733. The libretto, in two acts, is by Jacopo Angello Nelli. The story is of the simplest: a maid creates a fictitious suitor to make her master jealous, and the master quickly marries the maid. There are only three characters—a male singer (the master), a female singer (the servant), and a mute (the fictitious suitor). There is no chorus or ballet.

The opera was an immediate success, and was indeed the first comic opera to be performed all over the world. It did not always win success in foreign countries at once. When it was first performed in Paris on October 4, 1746, it met a cold reception, but when it was performed again in 1752 it was received with enthusiasm.

La Serva Padrona has been likened to Mozart's *The Marriage of Figaro*. There is similarity of quickness of movement, absurdity of story, and tonal color. The music of Mozart, however, is more supple and is not quite so superficial.

Pergolesi wrote other comic operas of quality, among them *Livietta e Tracollo* and *Il Maestro di Musica.* According to some authorities they are as good as *La Serva Padrona.*

The twenty-six-year-old Pergolesi did nothing less than establish a new art form. The *opera-buffa* became the *opéra comique* in France and the *Singspiel* in Germany. And much later it became the musical comedy in America.

This lowly musical form has sufficient reason for its wide popularity: it has color, liveliness, and variety. It is a civilized form of carefree entertainment.

VI

Arcangelo Corelli, Antonio Vivaldi, Giuseppe Tartini, Dietrich Buxtehude

ARCANGELO CORELLI WAS THE father of modern violin-playing, and his concerto grosso was clearly the precursor of the concerti for solo violin and orchestra by Bach, Vivaldi, Handel and Tartini.

Not much is known about his personal life. He was born at Fusignano, near Ravenna, on February 17, 1653, and died in Rome on January 8, 1713. His teacher in counterpoint was Matteo Simonelli, and in the violin, G. B. Basani. He was so great a virtuoso on the violin at the age of seventeen that he was made a member of the celebrated Academia Filarmonica of Bologna. He served in the Court of Munich, and is known to have been in Paris and Hanover in 1672 or thereabout.

In 1675 he was in Rome, where he was third violinist in the orchestra of the Church of S. Luigi dei Francesi. In 1685 he published in Rome a set of twelve sonatas. His patron was Pietro Ottoboni who at the age of twenty-two was made a cardinal by his uncle, Pope

Arcangelo Corelli

Alexander VIII. Cardinal Ottoboni was a genuine lover of music, and Corelli resided at his palace from 1687 to the end of his life in 1713.

Corelli conducted the Cardinal's Monday concerts, which were an important social as well as musical event. His playing and composing became famous throughout Europe, and as a result he was made head of *Congregazione dei Musici di Roma sotto l'Invocazione di Santa Cecilia.*

Apparently he was a very simple and mild man. Even when he became wealthy he went about on foot, generally dressed in black. Ordinarily he had a calm expression, but when he played the violin, "his eyes blazed and he threw himself into convulsions."

He had among his pupils of violin-playing many who later became famous. Perhaps the most famous among them were Francesco Geminiani (1680-1762) and Pietro Locatelli (1693-1764). The first was known as the master of Dubourg and the second as the master of Leclair. Their pupils became the teachers of others and so on down to Vieuxtemps, Baillot, Léonard, and Sarasate. Corelli, therefore, according to Stanford, "was responsible for nearly all the outstanding violinists in Italy, France and Germany for two centuries."

Corelli's completed works fill only six volumes, but nearly every composition in it is at least neatly formed. He was a severe self-critic.

According to Nef, Corelli was without question "the first to create a definite sonata form. . . . Put briefly, it is the form, slow-fast-slow-fast, which lies at the basis of this older sonata form, and which prevailed until the middle of the eighteenth century." Thereafter the form was altered to fast-slow-fast. "Corelli himself not only determined the form, but in his solo sonatas and trio sonatas also created works of art of significant content, which, especially on account of their genuine violin character, will remain models for all time."

The qualities of Corelli's works are clarity and compression, force and elegance. His suites are models of their kind. The slow movements are particularly happy; they have a majesty all their own.

His concerti grossi, which fill one volume, are of special significance. Corelli apparently looked upon them as his greatest work, for he was forever revising them. Unlike the three-movement concerti by Stradella and Torelli, Corelli's are in five or six movements. According to Prunières' analysis, Corelli "observes no rigid rule for the succession of movements, nor for their development. Concerned with dramatic and picturesque expression, he devises contrasts of color between the various sections."

Lully clearly influenced Corelli, especially in his writing of gavottes and minuets. "This accounts to some extent for Corelli's exceptional success with the

French musicians. The whole French violin school may be said to have issued from his work, while Couperin's constant aim was to mate the style of Corelli with that of Lully."

One of the best known of Corelli's concerti grossi is the Christmas Concerto, Op. 6, No. 8, in G minor. A musical description of the Nativity, it contains a Pastorale that is one of the loftiest expressions of religious feeling in music.

Purcell was so impressed with the music of Corelli that he attempted to "imitate" him. Corelli's influence upon Handel was even more marked.

Antonio Vivaldi carried the virtuosity of Corelli still further, and in his compositions for the violin perhaps surpassed his predecessor. He had done enough himself in the realm of music to assure himself a firm place in the history of the art, but his place became doubly assured when the mighty Johann Sebastian Bach arranged some of his works for the clavichord, the organ and the string quartet.

Vivaldi was born in Venice in 1675, and died there in poverty in 1743. He was the son and pupil of Giovanni Battista Vivaldi, an eminent musician. Because of the color of his hair the young Vivaldi was often called *il prete rosso*, or redhead.

One of the greatest violinists of his time, he was long director of the *Ospedale della Pieta*, or Conserv-

LR

Antonio Vivaldi

atory for Girls, in Venice. He became a priest in 1703, but his health was so poor that he was excused from saying Mass.

Nevertheless, he was always busy playing and composing. He made many journeys to Rome, Vienna, and possibly Germany.

He wrote many operas and choral works. But he is chiefly remembered for his compositions for the violin. He wrote more than 100 concertos and sonatas for the violin, and also a great deal of chamber music, including many concerti grossi. Bach arranged sixteen of these concerti grossi for the clavichord, four for the organ, and one for four clavichords and string quartet.

The two major sets of concerti grossi are *L'Estro armonico* (Harmonic Inspiration) and *Il Cimento dell' Armonia e dell' Inventioni* (The Trial of Harmony and Invention). The first set, Op. 3, is made up of twelve works, and was first published in Amsterdam in 1714. The second is made up of eight works and was also published in Amsterdam, but the exact date is unknown.

Vivaldi revolutionized the concerto grosso by replacing the traditional concertante trio with the solo violin part. The orchestra served as background for the violin virtuoso.

Generally Vivaldi used three movements in his sonatas and concerti—allegro-largo-allegro. He brought fresh ideas to the composition of the orchestra. He gave new importance to horns and oboes. Hitherto they generally doubled the violins; now they accented and punctuated the speech of the string section.

Some critics and historians look down upon Vivaldi's music as lacking in grace and charm and as being showy. Others, however, see in it some of the most beautiful pages in the annals of music. Prunières, for instance, says of him and his works:

"His flowing counterpoint is a marvel of rhythmic energy and harmonic power. . . . Some of the slow movements in the concerti and in the violin and cello sonatas are as sublime as anything in music."

Another important successor of Corelli's was Giuseppe Tartini who inaugurated a new era in the development of violin-playing, especially in digital technique and in bowing. As a composer he also brought great breadth and sometimes considerable profundity to his themes. Finally, he discovered resultant or partial notes, and thus won for himself a place in the history of physics.

Tartini was born in Pirano, Istria, on April 8, 1692, and died in Padua on February 26, 1770. He studied at the Collegio dei Padri delle Scuole pie in Capo d'Istria. For a time he thought of becoming a priest, and then a lawyer, but his natural inclinations led him inevitably into music.

Giuseppe Tartini

At an early age he made a runaway marriage and to get away from the police he fled to the monastery of Assisi. There he wrote "The Devil's Trill Sonata," which he claimed was a reproduction of a sonata played for him by the devil himself in a dream:

"One night in 1713 I dreamt that I had made a compact with the Devil. He promised to do what I wanted him to do. . . . I wondered what sort of musician he was, so I gave him my violin. Lo and behold he played a solo so divinely beautiful and with such skill that it surpassed any music I had ever heard before, or that I had imagined was possible. I was so overcome with my surprise and delight that I lost my power of breathing, and the violence of the sensation awoke me. Instantly I seized my violin in the hope of remembering some portion of what I had heard, but in vain! The work which this dream suggested, and which I wrote at the time, is doubtless the best of my compositions. I call it 'The Devil's Trill Sonata.' "

The sonata is in four movements and is filled with delicate and lovely melodies, as well as with long sprightly passages.

About the time of the composition of "The Devil's Trill" Tartini decided upon using thicker strings in the violin and improving the bow. Tartini played regularly at the chapel of the monastery that had given him refuge. He was shielded from the view of the public by a curtain. Hence no one knew his identity, though his concerts became famous in the vicinity.

It was not long before his identity was revealed when a deacon accidentally pulled aside the curtain. The officials of Padua decided to drop the charges against him. As a result Tartini and his wife were reunited. At Padua his fame increased so much that he was called outside Italy, and it is known that he was conductor of Count Kinsky's Orchestra in Prague.

In 1728 he founded his own school of violin-playing in Padua. Among his pupils were Nardini, Ferrari, Pasqualino Bino, Manfredi, Pagin, Graun, and Carminato.

He left a great many works—sonatas for the violin and clavichord, violin concerti, trios and concertos. He also wrote several historical and theoretical works.

The man to whom Johann Sebastian Bach was probably most indebted was Dietrich Buxtehude, a celebrated Swedish organist and composer. He was born in Helsingborg, Sweden, in 1637, and died in Lübeck in 1707. His father Johann Buxtehude was a Danish organist for the greater part of his life.

In 1668 Dietrich Buxtehude was made organist at the Marienkirche in Lübeck, and remained there for the remainder of his days. His virtuosity on the organ was almost miraculous. His fame spread to all parts of Europe and musicians traveled from far to hear him. Bach walked 200 miles to hear him and study under him.

In 1673 Buxtehude reorganized the services at the Marienkirche and improved them to such an extent that Lübeck became the musical Mecca of the continent.

Next to Bach he was perhaps the greatest composer for the organ. As an improviser he may well have been even greater. His works for the organ occupy an entire library. He wrote fantasias, choral preludes, fugues, chaconnes, passacaglias. One of his most important innovations was the composition of "free" organ music —that is, organ music free from the chorale tune as the central subject.

Of Buxtehude's choral prelude Cecil Gray has said that it "was raised to an unexemplified pitch of elaboration and enriched with every conceivable device of contrapuntal and decorative resource at his disposal."

A. Eaglefield Hull has said, "As John the Baptist was to Christ, so was . . . Buxtehude to Bach."

And the great Parry has written: "In Johann Sebastian Bach's works the traces of the influence of Buxtehude are more plentiful than those of any other composer. It is not too much to say that unless Dietrich Buxtehude had gone before, the world would have had to do without some of the most lovable and interesting traits in the divinest and most exquisitely human of all composers."

A complete edition of Buxtehude's organ works appeared in 1876-1878, under the editorship of P. Spitta.

About this time there lived a distinguished line of church composers who, while not of the first magnitude, contributed much to the musical life of their time. Among them were the following: Franz Tunder (1614-1667), Matthias Weckmann (1621-1674), Johann Schop (who died about 1665), Johann Crüger (1598-1662), Johann Rudolf Ahle (1625-1673), and Johann Sebastiani (1622-1683). The last was the Königsberg kapellmeister, who was probably the first to compose the "Passion" as an oratorio, a form that Bach later employed to the glory of religious music.

VII

Georg Friedrich Handel

GEORG FRIEDRICH HANDEL WAS one of the major links between the classical period and the modern period. He carried within his art the great contributions of such men as Monteverdi and Corelli, and he initiated new developments of his own, which form a part of the foundation of the work of modern composers

Of his art few have ever spoken in disparagement. The celebrated American critic, Philip Hale, who wrote the excellent program notes of the Boston Symphony Orchestra and was the music critic of the Boston *Herald*, said of him:

"This giant of a man could express a tenderness known only to him and Mozart. . . . No one has approached him in his sublimely solemn moments! Few composers, if there is anyone, have been able to produce such pathetic or sublime effects by simple means, by a few chords even. He was one of the greatest melodists. His fugal pages seldom seem labored; they are distinguished by amazing vitality and spontaneity. In his slow movements, his instrumental airs, there is a peculiar dignity, a peculiar serenity, and a direct appeal that we find in no other composer."

As his music was, his personal life was. Handel, said John F. Runciman, "is by far the most superb personage one meets in the history of music. He alone, of all musicians, lived his life straight through in the grand manner."

Handel was born about a month before Johann Sebastian Bach, on February 23, 1685, at Halle. He was the son of a surgeon and *valet de chambre* to Prince Augustus of Saxony and later to the court of Brandenburg. The composer's mother, Dorothea Taust, was his father's second wife. His father was about sixty-four at the time of the composer's birth, while his mother was in her early thirties. The elder Handel was in comfortable circumstances, though not wealthy. His wife was "clear-minded, of strong piety, with a great knowledge of the Bible; deeply attached to her parents; with little wish for marriage, even in the bloom of her youth; a capable manager, earnest and of pleasant manners."

Even in the nursery, it seems, the baby Handel was attracted by musical objects such as trumpets, flutes, drums, etc. When this interest persisted into late babyhood the elder Handel was deeply disturbed, for while he admitted that music was "an elegant art and a fine amusement; yet, if considered as an occupation, it had little dignity as having for its subject nothing better than mere pleasure and entertainment."

But try as the elder Handel would to keep music out of his son's mind, he could not keep him from hearing it. There was, first of all, the music heard in church; then there was the music performed by the church and town musicians weekly in the streets of Halle. The street music of those days was not of the lowly character heard nowadays. It was generally of a high order and the players and singers were very well trained, most of them in the service of the local church or the municipal authorities.

Young Handel heard all this music with an eager ear and a leaping heart. He must have been profoundly moved. There is a legend that before he was seven he managed to carry a small clavichord to the garret of his home and taught himself to play on it. Whether the story is true or not, it is definitely known that by the age of seven he astonished people with his musical talent.

It was obvious by now that it would be wise to give Handel some musical instruction, and his father reluctantly consented that he be given instruction by Friedrich Wilhelm Zachau, organist of the Liebfrauenkirche. Zachau taught him organ, counterpoint and composition. Handel was with him three years and near the end of this period was composing a motet or cantata a week. Unfortunately, none of these early works has been unearthed thus far.

About this time Handel also studied the harpsichord, the violin and the oboe, and sometimes substituted for Zachau at the organ. Handel's father, however, did not give up hope altogether that his son would lose interest in music. He managed to get him to become a law student at the University of Halle in 1702. It wasn't many weeks later, however, that Handel succeeded Johann Christoph Leporin as organist of the castle and the cathedral, and while Handel continued studying law for a few more months, it was clear to all now that music was to be his lifework.

When Handel accepted the post of organist he was given the usual instructions and admonitions, which were as follows, according to C. F. Abdy Williams, author of what is perhaps still the best one-volume biography of the composer:

"He was to fulfill the duties entrusted to him in a way becoming a competent organist, with faithful and diligent care; to be present on Sundays and festivals, and as any extra occasions require; to play the organ properly, to play over the psalm or hymn tune with fine harmony; to come in good time to the church; to look after the organ; to give advice as to any necessary repairs; to give due respect to priests and elders of the church; to be obedient to them, and to live peaceably with the church attendants; and to lead a Christian and exemplary life."

Handel was not offered the job outright. He was put on probation for a year. He served his probation year well. In that time he became acquainted with Georg Philipp Telemann, who later became one of the greatest church musicians of his day. Telemann, like Handel, had to endure the study of law for a while, before he was permitted to pursue music.

In his year of probation at the Halle cathedral Handel probably composed several score cantatas, not one of which is extant.

In the summer of 1703 Handel decided he could learn nothing more at Halle, so he left for Hamburg. Here he met Johann Mattheson, a gifted young man who helped Handel get pupils and engagements. On August 17, 1703 Handel and Mattheson went to Lübeck, forty miles away from Hamburg. Word had reached them that the aged organist there, Dietrich Buxtehude, organist of the Marienkirche, wanted to retire but he insisted that his successor marry his daughter, Anna Margreta, who was ten years older than Handel and six years older than Mattheson. Buxtehude himself had married the daughter of his predecessor. Apparently it was the expected thing for an organist or cantor to marry the daughter or widow of his predecessor.

Handel and Mattheson would have nothing to do

with the daughter. Mattheson tells of the experience thus:

"I took Handel with me; we played on all the organs and clavicymbals there, and finally agreed that he should only play on the organ and I only on the clavicymbal. We listened with much attention to good artists in the Marienkirche. But, as a matrimonial alliance was proposed in the business, for which neither of us had the slightest inclination, we departed, after receiving many tokens of esteem, and having had much enjoyment."

Johann Sebastian Bach also turned down the offer, and for the same reason, in 1705. A husband was finally found for Anna Margreta in the person of Johann Christian Schiefferdecker, former cymbalist at the Hamburg Opera.

Handel and Mattheson returned to Hamburg, which after all was one of the music centers of the continent, and which they hoped would have something for them soon or late. On December 5, 1704, Mattheson's opera *Cleopatra* was performed. The occasion was the cause of a strange quarrel between him and Handel. Mattheson generally doubled as singer and harpsichord player; when he sang, Handel played. This time, apparently, Handel was so engrossed in playing that he failed or refused to let Mattheson play. Mattheson was enraged and boxed his friend's ears as they left the theater.

A duel with swords ensued in the market place. A crowd gathered. Since Handel was not skillful at this sort of thing, Mattheson had little difficulty in getting the best of him, and only a miracle saved Handel from grave injury. According to legend they publicly embraced after the duel and became even better friends than before. Indeed, they attended together the rehearsals of Handel's first opera, *Almira, Queen of Castile,* which was produced on January 8, 1705. The author of the libretto was Friedrich Feustking, the same theological student who wrote the libretto of Mattheson's *Cleopatra.*

A few words here about Mattheson, who was Handel's close friend in this period of his life and influenced him to a degree. When only nine he was a remarkable organ player and played the instrument at several churches. He also composed and sang songs of his own, and was an acceptable performer on the double bass, violin, flute and oboe. Like Handel he studied some law and also knew more than a little English, French and Italian. At eighteen he had his first opera, *Die Pleyaden,* produced in Hamburg, and he was a principal tenor at the operas of others. He wrote many other operas, oratorios, several Masses, sonatas, and chamber works.

He was also adept with his pen. He wrote several volumes in the realms of biography, science, criticism, acoustics and, of course, music. At his death at the age of eighty-three he had eighty-eight books to his credit. He had also been a fencer and dancer. It is easy to see why Handel, who liked the grand manner or any fair sample of it, was attracted to Mattheson.

Almira was little more than a series of arias and recitatives, tied together with the barest of plots. It was an enormous success. It was performed continuously till February 25, something of a record for those days. It was immediately followed by Handel's second opera, *The Success of Love through Blood and Murder, or Nero*, with the words again by Feustking. It ran only three times.

Handel now occupied himself with teaching and playing the harpsichord in theaters. He decided to give up playing the second violin, which had hitherto helped support him. Always a frugal man, he saved his money and now could get along without help from his mother.

In 1708 Handel composed an opera that was so long it had to be divided into two—*Florindo* and *Daphne*. The score is lost. During this period Handel also composed a *Passion according to St. John* and "two chests full of cantatas, sonatas and other music," including harpsichord pieces and chamber works.

The Hamburg operas, incidentally, though written in German, had Italian arias, which was common practice in those days. Italian then was considered as perhaps the only language fit for musical treatment, while French and German were considered as suitable only for recitative.

In 1706 Handel went to Florence and Venice to augment his studies. In the latter city he met the two Scarlattis, Domenico and Alessandro, and Agostino Steffani, kapellmeister of the Hanover Opera House. Handel's reputation had preceded him, for he was already known as an excellent harpsichord player, organist and composer. The story is told that at a masked ball Handel played the harpsichord with such magnificence that Domenico Scarlatti exclaimed, "This must be either the famous Saxon or the Devil!" Handel had come to be referred to in Italy as "the famous Saxon."

In 1707 Handel wrote the music for two psalms, *Dixit Dominus* and *Laudate pueri,* and his first Italian opera, *Roderigo.* The following year he traveled further in Italy, and at Rome he met Corelli, whose music exerted a great influence upon him. Handel continued to write vast masses of music in almost every form, but perhaps the outstanding works of this period were oratorios and cantatas, among them *La Resurrezione, Il Trionfo del tempo e del disinganno, Apollo e Dafne* and *Fillide ed Aminta.* About thirty years later Handel reworked *Il Trionfo* into the English oratorio, *The Triumph of Time and Truth.* The characters were Beauty, Pleasure, Time and Truth.

On December 26, 1709, Handel's opera *Agrippina*

was produced in Venice. It is Handel at his opulent best—up to then. Its overture is full and dignified, and the chorus is accompanied by drums, trumpets and the usual strings. The opera created a sensation, and throughout the performance there were shouts of "Viva il caro Sassone!"

Representations were immediately made upon Handel to go to Hanover or England. Steffani prevailed upon him to go to Hanover, where, apparently through Steffani's own intervention, Handel was appointed successor to Steffani as Kapellmeister of the Hanoverian court, on June 16, 1710.

Men of station in England did not give up, however, in their endeavor to get Handel to their country. Opera had declined there. The death of Purcell—"the miniature Mozart of England"—had left the country without a worthy successor, and the music lovers of England were pretty much limited to bits of arias, intermezzi, or dance music from Italy.

Handel, perhaps seeing an opportunity for himself, was finally persuaded to go to England. He was presented to Queen Anne, and the impresarios at once began to work on him for an opera. Aaron Hill, director of the Haymarket Theatre, persuaded Handel to write an opera to a book by Giacomo Rossi. He performed the feat in two weeks, and *Rinaldo* was produced on February 24, 1711. It must be pointed out that Handel used several earlier arias and recitatives of his; the speed of composition was remarkable nevertheless.

Rinaldo was an immediate success. One of the airs, *Cara Sposa,* a special favorite of the composer's, swept the country into almost every home where there was a harpsichord and an acceptable singing voice. The march was adopted by the British Life Guards, and about twenty years later became the highwayman's chorus in *The Beggar's Opera.* The publisher of *Rinaldo,* one Walsh, made the equivalent of $10,000 on it, which was much less than Handel made. It is reported that Handel told Walsh that they exchange roles in the next opera—that Walsh compose it and Handel do the selling. *Rinaldo* was later produced in Italy and Germany.

Handel returned for a while to Germany, where he composed several oboe concerti and cantatas. He yearned to be back in England. He had promised Queen Anne to return as soon as possible, and he discovered that he meant it more than he realized at the time. He liked the English people and their ways, and it seemed to him that they understood and appreciated his music. He remained in England, except for an occasional trip to Germany, for the rest of his life.

No doubt one of the things that kept on returning to Handel's mind was the concert room of the remarkable Thomas Britton. There was no man quite like him, in all probability, anywhere else in Europe. According to Williams he made his living "by selling coal about the streets, at first carried in sacks on his back, later pushed from house to house on a barrow. When his daily round was finished he went home to his shop near Clerkenwell Green, changed his clothes, and was then ready to receive his company. He was a most enthusiastic collector of music and musical books. He converted the long, low loft over his shop into a regular concert room, in which were all kinds of instruments, including a small organ. For some thirty years this room, which could only be approached by a narrow outside staircase, and was 'so mean in every respect as to be only a fit habitation for a very poor man,' was the weekly resort of all musical amateurs of whatever wealth or rank, and of all professional musicians. Britton made no charge for his concerts; all who came were his guests."

Handel came there often, played the organ, met several prominent musical and literary figures, and in general spent a pleasant time.

On his return to London late in 1712 Handel produced an opera, *Il Pastor Fido*. It was a failure. He accepted the invitation of the Earl of Burlington to live at his home. Here, apparently, he became acquainted with Gay, Pope, Arbuthnot, and other literary celebrities.

In the summer of 1713 Handel composed a *Te*

Deum and Jubilate for the celebration of the Peace of Utrecht. Queen Anne rewarded Handel with an annual pension of £200. Since Handel was already receiving an annual salary of £300 from the Hanoverian court and was living at the home of the Earl of Burlington, he had no financial worries. All he had to do at the Earl's home was to direct his concerts.

In 1714 Queen Anne died, and was succeeded by the Elector of Hanover, who became George I of England. The new king had been Handel's employer in Hanover. Since Handel had been absent from the Hanoverian court for so long, there was some unfriendly feeling between the monarch and the composer. This feeling, however, did not last long. According to legend it was Handel's *Water Music* which so captivated the King that he decided to "forgive" the composer, but there is no proof for this. What probably happened is that the King, who had long admired Handel's work, decided to rise above whatever petty resentment he harbored.

The *Water Music* is a charming instrumental group, scored for four violins, one 'cello, one viol, one double bass, two oboes, two bassoons, two horns, two flageolets, one trumpet, and one flute. It is still one of Handel's most popular instrumental works.

In 1717 Handel was made musical director for the Duke of Chandos. Here he wrote the twelve Chandos Anthems for solos and small chorus, the serenata (or

Georg Friedrich Handel

pastoral) *Acis and Galatea* (to words by John Gay), and the masque *Hamman and Mordecai*, which later became the oratorio *Esther*.

In 1720 appeared Handel's first instrumental publication. It was called *Suites de Pièces pour le Clavecin*. It is a chaconne with sixty-two variations, and it was quickly reprinted, to popular acclaim, in Germany, Holland, Switzerland, and France. The preface to the work ran as follows:

"I have been obliged to publish some of the following lessons, because surreptitious and incorrect copies of them had got abroad. I have added several new ones to make the work more useful, which if it meets with a favorable reception, I will still proceed to publish more, reckoning it my duty, with my small talent, to serve a nation from which I have received so generous a protection."

The group of variations known as the *Harmonious Blacksmith* appears in this suite. No one really knows how the name got attached to this group of variations. Handel did not use it. The traditional explanation is that Handel picked up the tune in a blacksmith's shop, whither he had gone to seek shelter from the rain. But there is no proof of this explanation or of any other explanation.

About this time Handel joined with Giovanni Maria Bononcini and Attilio Ariosti in the direction of a new operatic venture, the Royal Academy of

Music. On April 27, 1720, Handel's opera *Radamisto* (to a book by Haym) was performed at the Academy to an enthusiastic audience. Charles Burney said of the opera: It is "more solid, ingenious and full of fire than any drama which Handel had yet produced in this country. And John Mainwaring reports that there was an enormous crowd present:

"In so splendid and fashionable an assembly of ladies (to the excellence of their taste we must impute it), scarce indeed any appearance of order or regularity, politeness or decency. Many who had forced their way into the house with an impetuosity but ill-suited to their rank and sex, actually fainted through the heat and closeness of it. Several gentlemen were turned back who had offered forty shillings for a seat in the gallery, after having despaired of getting any seat in the pit or boxes."

The story of the opera derives from Tacitus' *Annals* and is little more than a thread for the arias, recitatives and choruses.

Soon jealousy entered into the ranks of the three directors of the Royal Academy of Music. The partisans of Bononcini attempted to show that he was a more popular composer than Handel and vice versa. Handel and Bononcini were at first friendly rivals who enjoyed almost equal success. But apparently the ill-feeling of their separate admirers managed to cool their friendship, especially when jingles of the following nature began to appear in London:

> "Some say, compared to Bononcini,
> That Mynherr Handel's but a ninny;
> Others aver, that he to Handel
> Is scarcely fit to hold a candle.
> Strange all this difference should be
> 'Twixt Tweedledum and Tweedledee."

The venture finally collapsed, but the financial damage to Handel was not very large. It is true that several of his published musical works were pirated, in accordance with the custom of the times (there was no property right, in those days, in literary or musical works), but he had been frugal and had been fairly regularly employed as teacher or conductor. By and large he was well satisfied with his stay in England. On February 14, 1726, he became a naturalized British subject.

Soon Handel was busy in a new operatic venture, and he went to Europe, especially Italy, to find singers. On this trip he saw his mother for the last time, and it was during the same trip that Bach invited him for a visit to Leipzig. Bach himself was too ill to go to Halle. Handel, finding his mother blind and dying, had to refuse Bach's invitation. They never did meet.

On his return to England Handel produced two of

his latest operas, *Lotario* and *Partenope*, on December 2, 1729, and February 24, 1730, respectively. Both were failures. And again Handel and his music were subjected to ridicule and worse. The following is a sample lampoon:

"In days of old when Englishmen were men,
Their music like themselves was grave and plain.

* * *

In tunes from sire to son delivered down,
But now, since Britons are become polite,
Since masquerades and operas made their entry,
And Heydegger and Handell ruled our gentry;
A hundred different instruments combine,
And foreign songsters in the concert join
And give us sound and show, instead of sense."

Handel attempted to recoup his reputation with a new opera, *Deborah*, which was put on in the spring of 1733. The *Daily Journal* of London made the following announcement:

"By His Majesty's command, *Deborah*, an oratorio or sacred drama in English, composed by Mr. Handel. The house to be fitted up and illuminated in a new and particular manner; and to be performed by a great number of the best voices and instruments."

This work, too, was a failure. And once again Handel was the subject of ridicule and satire. There were many, however, who had only high praise for the composer. Dr. Arbuthnot wrote a booklet, *Harmony in an Uproar: a Letter to Frederick Handel, Esq.*, in which he made these charges against Handel:

"Imprimis, you are charged with having bewitched us for the space of twenty years past. Secondly, you have most insolently dared to give us good musick and harmony, when we wanted and desired bad. Thirdly, you have most feloniously and arrogantly assumed to yourself an uncontrolled property of pleasing us, whether we would or no; and have often been so bold as to charm us when we were positively resolved to be out of humour. . . .

"Have you taken your degrees? Are you a doctor? A fine composer, indeed, and not a graduate. . . . Why, Dr. Pushpin and Dr. Blue laugh at you, and scorn to keep you company. . . . You have made such musick as never man did before you, nor, I believe, never will be thought of again when you are gone, etc., etc."

Pope once asked Dr. Arbuthnot what he really thought of Handel as a composer, and Dr. Arbuthnot answered: "Conceive the highest that you can of his abilities, and they are much beyond anything that you can conceive."

Handel's health was beginning to decline and he went to Aix-la-Chapelle in the hope of getting better. He improved considerably, and in 1739 he produced *Saul* and *Israel in Egypt.* In the winter of 1741

Handel went to Dublin where he gave a series of highly successful concerts of organ music and chamber music, as well as several vocal pieces. One periodical said these concerts were "superior to anything of the kind in the kingdom before." His popularity grew and grew and soon "the entertainments had become so popular that it was found necessary to regulate the traffic, to hire a convenient room for the footmen and to make a new passage for sedan-chairs."

On March 27, 1742 appeared the following notice in *Faulkner's Journal* of Dublin:

"For the relief of the prisoners in the several gaols, and for the support of Mercer's Hospital, and the Charitable Infirmary, on Monday the 12th of April will be performed at the Musick Hall in Fishamble Street, Mr. Handel's grand new oratorio, called *The Messiah*, in which the gentlemen of the choirs of both cathedrals will assist, with some concertos on the organ by Handel."

The three Dublin papers were highly enthusiastic. One said:

"The best judges allowed it to be the most finished piece of music. Words are wanting to express the delight it afforded to the admiring, crowded audience. The sublime, the grand, and the tender, adapted to the most elevated, majestic and moving words, conspired to transport and charm the ravished heart and ear."

When *The Messiah* was performed in London the next year it was a failure. The oratorio, in fact, did not become popular in that city till about 1750. Handel apparently was so shocked by the initial London failure that he took to bed, and his recovery was not at all hastened by the scurrilous attacks upon him, his music, and even his morals, which persisted.

His eyesight was beginning to fail him, his general health was sinking steadily, his finances were not what they should be, yet he kept on working, and he wrote several more operas, oratorios, and instrumental pieces: the *Dettingen Te Deum, Joseph, Semele, Belshazzar, Judas Maccabeus, Joshua, Solomon* and *Theodora.* He then began work on his last major oratorio, *Jephtha.* He could barely see what he was writing. He submitted to a serious operation upon his eyes:

"His spirits forsook him, and that fortitude which had supported him under afflictions of another kind deserted him in this, scarce leaving him patience to wait for that crisis in his disorder in which he might hope for relief. . . . Repeated attempts to relieve him were fruitless, and he was given to expect that freedom from pain in the visual organs was all that he had to hope for the remainder of his days. As he could now no longer conduct his oratorios, he called upon Smith, the son of his amanuensis, to assist him, while he was forced to confine himself to extempore voluntaries on the organ."

Soon he became almost totally blind. He could write no more new works. He spent such energy as he had chiefly in revising old works. Occasionally he appeared at concerts, playing the harpsichord and the organ from memory.

On April 6, 1759, he conducted, while playing the organ, a performance of *The Messiah* at Covent Garden. He never appeared in public again. He died on April 14, 1759. He was buried in Westminster Abbey on April 20.

Handel left an enormous amount of music in almost every form. Among his vocal works are sixty operas, numerous serenatos, odes, cantatas, French and German songs, twenty-five oratorios and passions, many anthems and a large number of motets and hymns. His instrumental music was not so plentiful: the *Water Music*, the *Firework Music*, the *Forest Music*, three suites, six fugues, a number of concertos and sonatas for the organ, oboe, and viola.

In the main his music was very much like the man, pleasant, easy-going, aristocratic, and at times majestic. Always it has quality, and sometimes it has size. "He was in his person a large made, and very portly man. . . . His features were finely marked, and the general cast of his countenance placid, bespeaking dignity attempered with benevolence, and every quality of the heart that has a tendency to beget confidence and insure esteem."

Handel's operas are now pretty much forgotten. There are, however, passages in them that deserve remembering. The most popular is the so-called *Largo*, which is the aria *"Ombra mai fu"* in the opera *Xerxes*. Williams has said:

"Handel was not a reformer like Gluck and Wagner. He took the opera as he found it and simply embellished it by means of his great genius. . . . Handel, in his operas, was essentially a man of his own times. He made no effort to advance the art; he simply took the forms he found ready-made and adorned them with all the beauty and solidity he was capable of producing, which far surpassed the operatic efforts of his contemporaries. He did not anticipate future developments; his effort was to attract his own public by the best possible art that he could give them."

The subject matter of Handel's operas is a definite obstacle to their present-day popularity. They deal with classical themes in a stereotyped manner—and the stereotyped manner of a bygone time. The difficulty of the singing parts also stands in the way of Handel's present-day popularity. Too many of the parts are written for male sopranos, a type now extinct. These facts, plus a general change in operatic tastes, account for the almost total eclipse of Handel's operas.

Handel wrote many church pieces, but he cannot

be called a church composer. His anthems and hymns and *Te Deums* are too earthly. But in the realm of the oratorio Handel was magnificent—indeed, he was perhaps the greatest composer of oratorios in all musical history. His oratorios have melody, counterpoint, harmony, deep feeling—all blended into a towering mass of sheer musical magic.

And of all of Handel's oratorios, *The Messiah* is easily the most sublime. Not a year passes that it is not performed in almost every Christian church that has the singers and the facilities to present it. The celebrated "Hallelujah Chorus" is one of the pinnacles of human creation. In the words of Prunières, it is "a joyous clamor to the heavens." According to Williams, "The highest ideals of the Christian religion are here set forth and enhanced by music which in its strength, its sincerity and its entire fitness to the subject appeals to learned and unlearned with equal force."

The miracle is that Handel wrote this glorious work in twenty-two days, and that at the time he was in the depths of personal misery and bankruptcy. Like Beethoven he was seldom hampered creatively by worldly troubles. And like Mozart he wrote at white heat when the spirit moved him. Says Newman Flower:

"It was the achievement of a giant inspired. Handel was unconscious of the world during that time, unconscious of its press and call. His whole mind was

in a trance. He did not leave the house: his man servant brought him food, and as often as not returned in
an hour to the room to find the food untouched, and
his master staring into vacancy. When he had completed Part II, with the 'Hallelujah Chorus,' his servant found him at the table, tears streaming from his
eyes. 'I did think I did see all Heaven before me, and
the great God Himself!' he exclaimed. . . . Never in
his life had he experienced the same emotional sense,
and he never experienced it again."

Handel's instrumental music is not so important as
his oratorios. Nef says that Handel is the "classic
representative of the clavier suite, and can be placed
beside Bach." This is an extreme view. Most critics
incline to the view that Handel's compositions for the
harpsichord, for the violin, for the viola, and for the
'cello are facile rather than inspired.

His concerti grossi have greater value than his
sonatas. He himself thought so highly of them that
he published them himself. They are "impression-
istic" music in the finest sense. They have grace and
tenderness and, occasionally, otherworldliness. Handel's concerti grossi were in the Italian tradition. They
were dialogues between a group of soloists (usually
two solo violins and a solo 'cello)—known as the
concertino—and the orchestral background—known
as the *concerto grosso*.

A special word must be said about Handel's concertos for the organ. He had a special fondness for that king of musical instruments. He improvised on it frequently and at great length. Some of the concertos for organ are often played on the harpsichord. Altogether Handel composed three volumes of concertos for the organ. Two of them were published in his lifetime.

Perhaps the most popular of Handel's purely instrumental music is the suite known as the *Water Music*. It has six movements: allegro, air, bouree, hornpipe, andante, and allegro deciso. They are all written with impeccable taste and great skill, and the effect of the whole is that of inexpressible loveliness and charm.

Joyousness, freedom of soul, depth of emotion— these three qualities perhaps best describe Handel and his music. Says Prunières: "Never was a creative genius more free. . . . There never was a composer less pedantic than Handel; everything he wrote was deeply felt."

VIII

Johann Sebastian Bach and Franz Joseph Haydn

THE CONSIDERATION OF JOHANN
Sebastian Bach and Joseph Haydn
does not strictly belong in this volume, since their
work, while deeply involved with that of their predecessors, points more in the direction of the future.
Besides, Bach was not as influential in his own time as
were Handel or Buxtehude and many others, and
Haydn lived well into the nineteenth century. But
it is fitting to say a few words about both these giants,
if only because they stand at the crossroads of musical
history.

Robert Schumann has said that "music owes as
much to Bach as religion to its Founder." The German musicologist Forkel, on rediscovering Bach in
1802, exclaimed, "This sublime genius, this prince of
musicians, German or foreign, dwarfs all others from
the heights of his lofty superiority."

Up to the time of Bach and Handel, who were
contemporaries, Germany was looked upon by the
Italians and French and even the English, as pretty

much of a barbaric land musically. There was sufficient truth in this belief to make intelligent Germans ashamed. The musical great for two centuries had generally been natives or residents of other lands. Handel changed this belief (and fact) in his own day, and Bach was the first to make a mockery of it for all time. Had Germany produced no other composer it could, with Bach, so to speak, look every other nation in the face with equanimity.

Johann Sebastian Bach came of a family that had produced musicians of quality for two centuries. He himself was born in Eisenach on March 31, 1685. His first teacher was his father, who gave him lessons on the violin. He also studied the organ and voice, and was a choir boy. For a while he was organist at Arnstadt, and here he wrote some of his first works. In 1706 he became organist to the court at Weimar. Here he remained for nine years, and continued to write, especially organ compositions.

Meanwhile he made concert tours throughout Germany and won a high reputation for himself as an organist, violinist, and harpsichord player, especially the first. He then moved to the court of Anhalt-Köthen, where he composed most of his chamber music. It was there that he wrote the first volume of *The Well-Tempered Clavichord*. In 1723 he got the position of cantor of St. Thomas Church in Leipzig.

Johann Sebastian Bach

Here he was to the end of his days, and here he wrote his monumental cantatas. He died in 1750.

His death made little impression on the contemporary musical world: only another musician had passed to his reward. The Leipzig *Chronicle* noted the death in the following brief notice:

"July 28, at eight in the evening, the learned musician, Herr Johann Sebastian Bach, composer of His Majesty the King of Poland, Kapellmeister to the courts of Gothen and Weissenfels, director and cantor of the school of St. Thomas, died."

His widow was left with eleven children—Bach was the father of twenty, but nine died during his lifetime—and quickly became the object of charity. When she died she was buried in a pauper's grave.

Bach's eminence as a player on the organ and clavichord, his most mortal contribution to music, was recognized in his own day. Even his enemies admitted his virtuosity. Landorny quotes one of them as follows:

"He is the most eminent among instrumental players. He is an extraordinary artist on the clavecin and on the organ, and has encountered but one musician who might pretend to rival him. At various times I have heard this great man play. One marvels at his dexterity, and it is hard to imagine it possible for him to cross his hands and feet in so unique and rapid a manner, to stretch them out and embrace the greatest intervals without the intermixture of a single false note, and without displacing his body, in spite of this violent agitation."

But as much as Bach's virtuosity was admired, his works were thought little of, and even sneered at. Contemporary critics decried his "pomposity," his "overladen style," "pedanticism," and even "compositorial awkwardness." The incredible blindness of his contemporaries is discussed in detail, with heavy documentation, in the excellent volume, *The Bach Reader*, edited by Hans T. David and Arthur Mendel. *The Art of the Fugue* was originally published in 1751, one year after the master's death. It sold only thirty copies during the next five years. His son, Carl Philipp Emanuel, was so disgusted that he offered the plates to the highest bidder. On September 15, 1756, he publicly announced:

"Publishers of practical musical art works are hereby notified of my decision to sell directly, at a reasonable price, the cleanly and accurately engraved copper plates of the fugal work (announced some years ago) by my late father, Capellmeister Joh. Seb. Bach. The number of the same comes to sixty odd, and they amount to about a hundredweight. Of the intrinsic value of this work it is unnecessary to say much, since the respect of connoisseurs of this kind of work for my late father, especially in the fugue, of whatsoever nature and form, is still not extinct.

But I may be permitted to observe this much: that it is the most perfect practical fugal work, and that every student of the art, with the help of a good theoretical instruction book, such as the one by Marpurg, must necessarily learn from it to make a good fugue, and thus needs for his instruction no oral teacher, who often charges dear enough for imparting the secret of the fugue."

Bach remained pretty much forgotten for fifty years. Mozart was perhaps the first eminent musician to hear Bach played after that length of time. One day in 1789 he was present in St. Thomas Church, Leipzig, and heard some Bach performed. He was so thrilled that he spread word of his discovery far and wide. A bit later Schumann and Mendelssohn, especially the latter, began to dig into the attics and cellars of Leipzig and other cities for Bach manuscripts and came up with invaluable findings. In 1850 the *Bachgesellschaft* (the Bach Society) was formed, and the systematic search for Bach material was begun. That search continues to this day.

The quantity of works unearthed so far is monumental. Merely listing them would take pages upon pages, and commenting upon them has occupied scholars and critics for more than one hundred years, and doubtless will continue to interest musicologists and critics for ages to come. He is the first among the first of musicians. There is hardly a musical form he did not enrich.

It is necessary, however, at least to refer to the most important of his compositions. Among his choral works are the *St. Matthew Passion*, the *St. John Passion*, the *Mass in B Minor*, the *Christmas Oratorio*, the *Peasant Cantata*, and the *Coffee Cantata*. Among his instrumental works surely these should at least be noted, even in this very rapid survey: the six *Branden-burg Concertos for Orchestra*, the *Concerto in the Italian Style*, the six Sonatas for violin and piano, the four suites for orchestra, the *Chromatic Fantasy and Fugue*, the two volumes of *The Well-Tempered Clavichord*, the six French suites, the six English suites, the thirty-two *Goldberg Variations*, *The Art of the Fugue*, the innumerable works for harpsichord, and the dozens of preludes, fugues, toccatas, partitas, and so on.

Bach was one of the most devout and modest of all composers. His basic principle of composition he expressed in these words: "The object of all music should be the glory of God." And while he was not unmindful of his own talents, he insisted that "any devout man could do as much as I have done, if he worked as hard."

Bach was a great scholar, humbly studying the works of such masters as Corelli, Vivaldi, and Bux-tehude. He always gratefully acknowledged his indebtedness to these men. But he did not stop with "borrowing." He built upon the work of these men and transformed their contributions so as to lift the art of music to new heights of glory. As David and Mendel observe:

"What is true of the monumental proportions, the contrapuntal intensity, the rhythmic consistency of Bach's works is just as true of the cogency of his themes, the expressiveness of his melodies, the force and richness of his harmony, the diversity and logic of his orchestration. In all of them he brought seeds well germinated by his predecessors to fruition on a scale undreamed of before him. And thus without any break with the past—in fact, as the great conservator of its legacies—Bach took what had been handed down to him and treated it with a boldness that often seemed almost revolutionary."

He transformed the pleasant cantatas of Buxtehude into tremendous orations to God, man, and history. He took the unaccompanied sonatas and partitas for violin and 'cello of such composers as Biber and Walther, and made of them virtual orchestral pieces. Through his development of music for the harpsichord and clavier he gave chamber music a push such as it had never had before—and he also gave it new stature. And his purely organ works, of course, became the fountain of inspiration for every organist who followed him.

The fugue is one of the most succinct and complex musical forms. It can speak the most profound musical thoughts—and it can also speak sheer musical dexterity. Bach always revealed the highest craftsmanship in his fugues, but he also, nearly always, had massive thoughts to communicate.

Perhaps, in the end, it will be his strictly religious works that will carry his name down the ages. These works, however, were religious in the most profound sense: they were a most intimate combination of poetry and philosophy cemented with sheer song. He probably wrote some three or four hundred religious cantatas—though only about two hundred are preserved —and in nearly every one of them there is musical beauty such as has never been equalled on this earth. Landormy says: "It is in his chorales, his choruses, and his recitatives that Johann Sebastian Bach is, perhaps, most grand, most profound, and also most equal to himself."

The only words that seem appropriate for the music of Bach are superlatives. He is not only the generally recognized highest peak of musical achievement; he stands as the keystone of musical history, holding the past and the future with firm and solid strength.

"Johann Sebastian Bach," says Landormy, "was a sort of monster; he unites within himself the opposing tendencies of several centuries, which he resumes or heralds. He derives from the Middle Ages through his polyphony and his love of description, is allied to the eighteenth century by his dramatic recitatives and his arias, and to the French seventeenth century by his elegance and his cultivation of ornament; while at the same time he prepares the gravid and somewhat ponderous, yet profound and puissant art of the aging Beethoven or Richard Wagner."

Bach had twenty children by his two wives—nine girls and eleven boys. Of the boys three were eminent composers in their own right: Wilhelm Friedman (1710-1784), Carl Philipp Emanuel (1714-1788), and Johann Christian (1735-1782). The second is frequently referred to as the father of the piano sonata, since he did so much to establish the three-movement form: fast-slow-fast. Both Mozart and Haydn were deeply indebted to him. Haydn said, "For what I know, I have to thank Philipp Emanuel Bach." Mozart went even further: "He is the father, and we his children. Those of us who know what is right have learned it from him; and those who have not confessed it are scoundrels."

Carl Philipp Emanuel's only teacher was his father. He first studied for the law, but gave it up for music. He was kapellmeister to Frederick the Great for many years, and in 1767 he succeeded Telemann as kapellmeister in Hamburg. For most of the eighteenth century in Europe he far surpassed his father in popularity and in critical acclaim.

Johann Christian was an organist of note. He wrote several masses and operas. In 1762 he went to England, where his operas and organ concerts won enthusiastic response. He became known as the "London Bach." But his music was not destined to endure, and today is virtually forgotten.

Franz Joseph Haydn's feet are even more in the field of modern music than those of Johann Sebastian Bach, but like Bach his work represents a culmination as well as a heralding. He was born in Rohrau, Austria, in 1732 and died in Vienna in 1809. As a boy he was a member of the choir of the celebrated St. Stephen's Church in Vienna, and for a time was an itinerant musician, playing the violin in the streets, in taverns, and in courts. He knew poverty and privation from his earliest years.

But always he studied music, and before long he was conducting a small orchestra in the court of Maximilian von Morzin, chamberlain to the Empress. Soon Haydn became musical director at the court of Prince Paul Anton Esterhazy, and there he remained the rest of his life. At the time he made this happy connection he made another one that brought him much unhappiness. He married the sister of the woman he really loved but who would not have him, and this mistake plagued him all his days. His wife turned out to be a monstrous shrew, with no understanding of her husband, his music, his friends or the world around her. Haydn, nevertheless, managed to build up a psychological defense against his domestic misery, so that his composition suffered very little, if at all.

He was a very prolific composer. His works include fourteen Masses, twenty-two arias, thirty-six songs, five grand operas, four comedies, many cantatas, including *Ariana a Naxos* and *The Ten Commandments*, and several oratorios, the most celebrated of which are *The Creation* and *The Seasons*. To these vocal works must also be added *The Seven Words from the Cross*. His instrumental works are far more numerous: at least 125 symphonies, including such well-known ones as the *Clock Symphony*, the *Surprise Symphony*, the *Farewell Symphony*, the *London Symphony*, the *Oxford Symphony*, the *Military Symphony*, and the *Toy Symphony*; seventy-seven string quartets, some forty piano trios, sixty-six works for wind and strings, a dozen collections of minuets, and about thirty concertos for various string instruments and orchestra.

As Karl Geiringer says, "Haydn, like Bach, was primarily a composer of instrumental music. . . . Haydn and Bach were forever *playing*; they thought in terms of instruments even if they wrote for voices."

Franz Joseph Haydn

He played a very important part in the shaping of
the classic sonata and symphony. He was not, of
course, the father of the sonata and the symphony, as
certain commentators long held. There were hundreds
of sonatas and symphonies before his day. But he so
improved the sonata form of Carl Philipp Emanuel
Bach that henceforth it became one of the most flexible of musical forms, and he definitely prepared the
way, in the realm of the symphony, for Mozart,
Beethoven, and even Brahms. He was a musical architect of supreme skill and grace, and as such definitely
placed the quartet, for the first time, on a firm foundation.

In content, his works tend to be pleasant, superficial,
and sometimes a little pointless—but hardly ever are
they dull. Haydn's temper, in the words of W. H.
Hadow, was "marked rather by feeling and imagina-
tion than by any sustained breadth of thought, and
hence, while they enrich their own field of art with
great beauty, there are certain frontiers which they
rarely cross, and from which, if crossed, they soon
return."

Or as J. Cuthbert Hadden has said, "To say that a
composition is 'Haydnish' is to express in one word
what is well understood by all intelligent amateurs.
Haydn's music is like his character—clear, straight-
forward, fresh and winning, without the slightest
trace of affectation or morbidity."

While Haydn was chiefly an instrumentalist, two of his vocal works deserve mention: *The Creation* and *The Seasons*. The book of the first is based upon Milton's *Paradise Lost*. It took Haydn a year and a half to finish it, and he was sixty-six when it was first performed in Vienna on April 29, 1798. It was an immediate success and was quickly produced all over Europe. Haydn was a deeply religious man and generally began and ended his manuscripts with "In nomine Deo" and "Laus Deo." The depth and sincerity of his religious feeling are apparent in *The Creation*, which is easily one of his greatest works. It is not profoundly philosophical or emotionally piercing as, say, Bach's *Mass in B Minor*, for Haydn was a different sort of man. But it is moving, occasionally robust, and gorgeously descriptive.

The Seasons is a series of tableaux in praise of God and His works. It makes charming listening. It was produced two years after *The Creation*.

A Bibliographical Note

IN THE WRITING OF THIS RAPID SUR-
vey of "pre-classical" music I have
consulted so many works over so long a period of time
that it is impossible for me to assay the full measure
of my indebtedness. I only hope at least in the text
I have stated all my authorities and given full credit
wherever it is due. If there has been any oversight it
has been wholly unintentional.

I hope the student will want to continue his study
of the men and movements considered in this volume.
If he does I trust he will find the following notes
helpful.

There are several excellent general histories of
music. Those I found very useful are these:

An Outline of the History of the Music, by Karl
Nef, late professor of musicology in the University
of Basel. Translated by Carl F. Pfatteicher, director
of music at Phillips Academy, Andover, Mass. Columbia University Press, New York, 1935.

A New History of Music. The Middle Ages to Mozart, by Henry Prunières. With an introduction by Romain Rolland. Translated from the French, and edited by Edward Lockspeiser. The Macmillan Company, New York, 1943.

A History of Music, by Paul Landormy. Translated, with a supplementary chapter on American Music, by Frederick H. Martens. Charles Scribner's Sons, New York, 1923.

A History of Music, by Charles Villiers Stanford and Cecil Forsyth. The Macmillan Company, New York, 1916.

All these books contain first-rate bibliographies.

A very popular but generally sound rapid survey is *Living Biographies of Great Composers*, by Henry Thomas and Dana Lee Thomas. Blue Ribbon Books, New York, 1946.

Special mention has to be made of *A Music Lover's Handbook*, edited by Elie Siegmeister. William Morrow and Company, New York, 1943. (It is a very good anthology of critical chapters by authorities in their respective fields.)

A useful bibliography is to be found in *Music for the Millions*, by David Ewen. Arco Publishing Company, New York, 1944. Mr. Ewen's individual chapters on musical masterpieces are generally good, and his phonograph record recommendations are enlight-

ened. Those searching for a good large or small encyclopedia of music will find his recommendations very
helpful. The classic encyclopedia, of course, is Sir
George Grove's *Dictionary of Music and Musicians.*
The Macmillan Company, New York, 1928.

The musical critical biographies in the Encyclopedia Britannica are of varying value. Many of them
are far too brief and many assume too great a previous
knowledge of musical history and criticism.

In the realm of sheer criticism mention surely
should be made of *Philip Hale's Boston Symphony
Programme Notes,* edited by John N. Burk, with an
Introduction by Lawrence Gilman. Doubleday, New
York, 1935. Philip Hale was for thirty-two years the
programme annotator of the Boston Symphony Orchestra and easily one of the best music critics this
country has ever produced. He died in 1934. The
younger student may find this volume heavy going at
times, but he will also find many shrewd observations
and much historical information that will be helpful.
There are good bibliographical notes throughout Mr.
Hale's pages.

I found *Handel,* by C. F. Abdy Williams, especially
good. It is published by E. P. Dutton, New York,
1935. It is one of the basic lives of this composer.

I also found many fine things in *Haydn. A Creative
Life in Music,* by Karl Geiringer. W. W. Norton &

Company, New York, 1946. The biographical section is perhaps better than the critical, but the whole work is a worthy one. The younger student, however, may find a good deal of it a bit too difficult.

For those who are fascinated by the evolution of musical taste and the strange changes in critical values, I recommend *Composer and Critic. Two Hundred Years of Musical Criticism*, by Max Graf. W. W. Norton & Company, New York, 1946. Mr. Graf was for many years an eminent Viennese music critic, and counted among his friends Brahms, Bruckner, and and Hugo Wolf. He has learning, humor, and humility.

For Bach lovers there is *The Bach Reader*, edited by Hans T. David and Arthur Mendel. W. W. Norton & Company, New York, 1945. There is more documentary information about Bach in this volume than in any other single study of him.

For those who live in New York City or nearby I wish to make special mention of the Fifty-eighth Street branch of the New York Public Library. It has one of the best musical libraries and record collections in the East. It is enriched almost annually with special collections donated by professional music critics and historians and lay music lovers. Those living at a distance from this library will find that their inquiries are answered promptly and courteously.

The Central Branch of the Boston Public Library is also excellent in its musical department.

The Music Section of the Library of Congress is, of course, the best in the country. Books from it may be borrowed by arrangement with one's local public library.

Recordings

THERE ARE SEVERAL GOOD BOOKS that deal with classical recordings. Some supply not only the necessary information about records, but also offer criticism. The beginning student, to whom this volume is chiefly addressed, need not concern himself too much with the variations in technical criticism. Some records, to be sure, are better, for various reasons, than others. But nearly all those produced by the better companies are of good general quality. Some record criticism has become over-fine, precious, and almost occult.

Here I list a few record books that are worth the attention of the student:

The Record Book, by David Hall. Citadel, 1946.

The Gramophone Shop Encyclopedia of Recorded Music. Simon & Schuster. 1942. This is a massive volume, and is largely for experts, but it is worth the student's time to browse through it, if only to obtain an idea what a rich field recorded classical music is.

Record Collector's Guide, by John Hines, Ben

Hyams, and Helmut Ripperger. Franklin Watts. 1947. This is a paper-covered book and sells for $1.00. It is probably the best of the less expensive record books. It covers not only classical records, but also folk song and jazz records. The classical section is a very good guide for beginning collectors in this field.

Then, as has been said in the bibliographical section, there are good record notes in David Ewen's *Music for the Millions*. Arco. 1944.

The record notations made here are based upon my own experience with particular records or upon the judgment of men and women who have also followed records over a number of years. The list is brief but selective. The student who wishes more extensive information can find it in the books listed above, or, indeed, in the comprehensive catalogues of the record companies.

CLAUDIO MONTEVERDI

The Nadia Boulanger Monteverdi Collection. A vocal ensemble. Madrigals and other works, with piano accompaniment by Nadia Boulanger. Victor Masterpiece 496.

Lagrime d'amante al sepolcro dell' amata. From the Sixth Book of Madrigals. The Cantori Bolognesi Chorus. Columbia Masterwork 218.

Ecco pur ch' a voi ritorno. From *Orfeo.* Ralph Crane. Victor 21747.

CHRISTOPH WILLIBALD GLUCK

Overture to Alceste. BBC Symphony. Boult. Victor 12041.

Alceste. Divinités du Styx. Traubel and Orchestra. Victor 17268.

Iphigenie en Aulide. Overture. CBS Symphony—Barlow. Columbia Masterwork X138.

Orphee et Eurydice. "Complete" opera in three acts. Vlassoff Orchestra and Symphony Orchestra—Tomasi. Columbia Masterwork set 15.

ALESSANDRO SCARLATTI

Se Florindo fedele. Aria from *Diana ed Endiminoe*. In Italian, Marian Anderson. Victor 17257.

Sonata a Quattro. Stuyvesant String Quartet. Columbia 17214D.

DOMENICO SCARLATTI

Fourteen Sonatinas for the Harpsichord. Yella Pessl. Columbia Masterwork 298.

Eleven Sonatinas for the Piano. Robert Casadesus. Columbia Masterwork 372.

JEAN BAPTISTE LULLY

Alceste Overture. Philadelphia Orchestra—Stokowski. Victor 7427.

Nocturne from Le Triomphe d'amour. Philadelphia Orchestra—Stokowski. Victor 7424.

Orchestral Excerpts from Four Operas. Atys. Amadis. Proserpine. Thésée. Columbia Masterwork 376.

Airs from Four Operas. Amadis. Armide et Renaud. Persée. Roland. Columbia Masterwork X117.

JEAN PHILIPPE RAMEAU

Suite in E Minor for the Harpsichord. Wanda Landowska. Victor Masterpiece 593.

Menuet Majeur & Menuet Mineur for the Harpsichord. Wanda Landowska. Victor 15179.

FRANÇOIS COUPERIN

Leçons de Ténèbres, No. 3 (Third Tenebrae Service for Holy Week). Women's Orchestra of Paris. Victor 12325.

La Sultane: Overture and Allegro. St. Louis Symphony—Golschman. Victor 11—8238.

Les Petits Moulins à Vent: La Soeur Monique; La Trophée. CBS Orchestra—Barlow. Columbia Masterwork X145.

HENRY PURCELL

Dido and Aeneas. Opera in 3 Acts. Soloists. Harpsichordist. Charles Kennedy Scott's A Capella Singers and the Boyd Neel String Ensemble. Clarence Raybould. Decca 25573-9.

Orchestral Selections from Dido and Aeneas. Philadelphia Orchestra—Ormandy. Victor Masterpiece 647.

Suite for Strings with Four Horns, Two Flutes and English Horn. New York Philharmonic-Symphony —Barbirolli. Victor Masterpiece 533.

GIOVANNI BATTISTA PERGOLESI

Stabat Mater. Vienna Choir with Hans Schneider, Erich Kurcher, harpsichordist, and string orchestra —V. Gomboz. Victor Masterpiece 545.

Sonata for Violin. No. 12 in E Major. Milstein. Columbia 69179D.

ARCANGELO CORELLI

Concerto Grosso No. 8 in G. Minor (Christmas Concerto). London Symphony—Walter. Victor Masterpiece 600.

Concerto for Organ and Strings in C and Sonata for Organ and Strings in D. E. Power Biggs with Arthur Fiedler Sinfonietta. Victor Masterpiece 924.

Suite for String Orchestra. Madrid Symphony Orchestra—Arbós. Columbia 68811D.

Sonata No. 8 in E Minor. Renardy. Columbia 69152.

ANTONIO VIVALDI

Concerto Grosso No. 11 in D Minor. Boston Symphony—Koussevitzky. Victor Masterpiece 886.

Concerto in A Major, No. 5 (L'Estro armonico). For string quartet. Pro-Arte. Victor 8827.

Concerto in G Minor. Elman. Symphony Orchestra—Collingwood. Victor 7585-6.

GIUSEPPE TARTINI

Sonata. Il Trillo del Diavolo. Milstein. Columbia Masterwork X98.

DIETRICH BUTEHUDE

Chorale Prelude. Ein Feste Burg. Weinrich. Musicraft 1050.

Collection of Chorale Preludes, Fantasies, and Fugues. Weinrich. Musicraft 40.

GEORG FRIEDRICH HANDEL

Concerto Grosso No. 6 in G Minor. London Symphony—Weingartner. Columbia Masterwork X154.

Harmonious Blacksmith. Wanda Landowska. Victor 1193.

The Messiah. Complete. BBC Chorus. London Symphony—Beecham. Columbia Masterwork 271.

The Water Music. London Philharmonic—Harty. Columbia Masterwork X14.

JOHANN SEBASTIAN BACH

Brandenburg Concertos Nos. 1-6. Busch Chamber Players. Columbia Masterwork 249-50.

Concerto for Two Violins and Orchestra in D Minor. Szigeti, Carl Flesch, with Harpsichordist and Orchestra—W. Goehr. Columbia Masterwork X90.

Fugue in G Minor (The Great). Philadelphia Orchestra—Stokowski. Victor 1728.

Fugue in G Minor (The Little). Philadelphia Orchestra—Stokowski. Victor 7437.

Mass in B Minor. Schumann, Balfour, Widdop, Schorr. Royal Choral Society. London Symphony—A. Coates. Victor Masterpiece 104.

KARL PHILIPP EMANUEL BACH

Concerto in D Major. Boston Symphony—Koussevitzky. Victor Masterpiece 559.

JOHANN CHRISTOPH BACH

Quartet No. 1 in E Flat Major. Perolé String Quartet. Musicraft 1003.

JOHANN CHRISTIAN BACH

Quartet for Flute and Strings in C Major. Oxford Ensemble. Musicraft 1039.

FRANZ JOSEF HAYDN

Quartet in B Flat Major. Op. 76. No. 4. (Sunrise). Pro-Arte. Victor Masterpiece 595.

Quartet in G Major. Op. 54. No. 1. Budapest. Victor Masterpiece 869.

Symphony in F Sharp Minor (Farewell). London Symphony—Wood. Columbia Masterwork 205.

Symphony in C Major (Toy). Weingartner. Columbia 7242.

Concerto for Harpsichord and Orchestra in D Major. Wanda Landowska. Symphony Orchestra—Bigot. Victor Masterpiece 471.

Symphony in G Major (Surprise). CBS Symphony—Barlow. Columbia Masterwork 363.

Students wishing to get better acquainted with pre-Monteverdi music will find the following records worth hearing:

GIOVANNI PIERLUIGI DA PALESTRINA

Missa Papae Marcelli. Westminster Cathedral Choir —Terry. (The first Agnus Dei is omitted from this recording). Victor 35941-4.

Hodie Christus Natus Est. Palestrina Choir—N. Montani. Columbia D17195.

Missa Brevis. The Mardigal Singers—Engel. Columbia Masterwork 299.

PLAINSONG

Gregorian Chants. Monks Choir of St. Pierre de Solesmes Abbey—Don J. Gajard, O.S.B. Victor Masterpiece 87.

Ordinary of the Mass. Pius X Choir, College of the

Sacred Heart—Justine B. Ward. Victor Masterpiece 69.

There is good early choral music in Victor Masterpiece 535, and good early organ music in Musicraft 9.
There is a generous number of Italian songs of the
seventeenth and eighteenth centuries in Victor Masterpiece 766.

Index